STIRRING UP
fun
with
food

STIRRING UP
fun
with
food

Over 115 Simple,
Delicious Ways to Be
Creative in the Kitchen

Sarah Michelle Gellar
AND GIA RUSSO

Photographs by Amy Neunsinger

GRAND CENTRAL
Life & Style
NEW YORK · BOSTON

Grand Central Life & Style
Hachette Book Group
1290 Avenue of the Americas
New York, NY 10104

www.GrandCentralLifeandStyle.com

Printed in the United States of America

Q-MA

First Edition: April 2017
10 9 8 7 6 5 4 3 2 1

Grand Central Life & Style is an imprint of Grand Central Publishing. The Grand Central
Life & Style name and logo are trademarks of Hachette Book Group, Inc.

The Hachette Speakers Bureau provides a wide range of authors for speaking events.
To find out more, go to www.HachetteSpeakersBureau.com or call (866) 376-6591.

The publisher is not responsible for websites (or their content) that
are not owned by the publisher.

Library of Congress Cataloging-in-Publication Data

Names: Gellar, Sarah Michelle, author. | Russo, Gia, author.
Title: Stirring up fun with food : over 115 simple, delicious ways to be creative
in the kitchen / Sarah Michelle Gellar and Gia Russo.
Description: First edition. | Grand Central Life & Style: New York, 2017. | Includes index.
Identifiers: LCCN 2016054252| ISBN 9781455538744 (hardcover edition) |
ISBN 9781455538737 (ebook edition) | ISBN 9781538760604 (signed edition)
Subjects: LCSH: Cooking. | Holiday cooking. | LCGFT: Cookbooks.
Classification: LCC TX714 .G445 2017 | DDC 641.5—dc23 LC record available at
https://lccn.loc.gov/2016054252

Sarah

First and foremost I want to dedicate this
book to MY FAMILY, who have supported me
through all of my crazy endeavors. Their love is the
safety net that allows me to pursue my dreams.

I also want to dedicate this book to my
INCREDIBLE FANS, who have followed me all
these years on this crazy journey. I couldn't do any of
this without you, nor would I want to.

Gia

To PETER and GRAYDEN for always inspiring
and supporting me. Love you...

To AUDRIANA—you are an inspiration.
Love you...

To my MOM, who has always been my rock—
Thank you! Love you...

Contents

July

October

August

November

September

December

INTRODUCTION

Most people know me as BUFFY the VAMPIRE SLAYER. The superhero. The role model.

EVEN HER TOMBSTONE READ, "She saved the world...a lot." I am also a wife, a mother, and—since I am writing this—an author.

Food and the experience of cooking mean something different to everyone, but to me they have always been about family. Mealtimes have always been when I "unplug" for a bit and engage in real, honest connections. Once I had kids, this experience became even more important. I wanted my kids not just to love food and to make healthy choices, but to experience the special bonding that happens in the kitchen and around the table.

How often do you hear "My kid doesn't eat vegetables" or "My kid only eats white food"? I was determined that I would never utter these phrases about my kids. And I knew from the start that I didn't want to hide ingredients. I wanted my children to know what they were eating, and through exploration, I believed they would learn to love different flavors (even Brussels sprouts—peeled apart, seasoned with a little truffle salt and shaved Parmesan cheese, and baked did the trick). By making them creative and fun, I was able to remove the stigma that vegetables weren't delicious.

I learned quickly that to get my kids to be adventurous with their choices, I had to involve them in the process of preparing food. Next came the tricky part. Unlike my husband, who went to culinary school, my related expertise thus far had been restricted to keeping up with the latest restaurants and making reservations at them. So I wound up learning about cooking with my kids, and sometimes even being taught a thing or two. What I initially thought would be intimidating became an adventure. In all honesty, at first I was worried that it was too late for me to learn, but I found the reality to be the exact opposite.

I discovered a new creative outlet that I was actually good at, and I realized that making fun food with my kids was about more than just getting them to eat. Measuring ingredients; pulling together pots, pans, and bowls; stirring, whisking, dumping, rolling, skewering—and waiting—are skills that helped them develop self-confidence, expand their vocabulary and creative thinking, and sharpen math concepts as well as their fine and gross motor skills (and mine too, for that matter).

But why food crafting? (And what exactly is food crafting, you might wonder?) As there is no truly acknowledged definition of food crafting, we will have to go with mine: →

Food crafting is taking basic food preparation and elevating it to a level that is both fun & creative.

Why stop at cutting brownies into squares? Why not put them on a stick and decorate them? Why not fold broccoli spears into a yummy cheesy muffin? Isn't it more fun to eat food out of a jar? I quickly realized that the possibilities for presenting were endless.

Now, don't get me wrong: not all my ideas were home runs. But creativity takes practice, and ultimately it leads to invention, so I just kept trying. (Someone once told me that the difference between success and failure is trying one more time. So true.)

FUN FOOD CAN ALSO COME THROUGH THE MAIL

~~~~~~

Three years ago, Gia and I and one of our best friends, and fellow mom, Galit Laibow, shared similar epiphanies: we were living in a society that was constantly becoming more digitally connected while at the same time becoming more and more domestically disconnected. We were reading more about breaking the Internet than breaking bread. It was disturbing. That's when we decided to embark on Foodstirs, our brand devoted to creating better-tasting and better-quality products that would encourage true connections in the kitchen.

We spent a full year creating our signature organic baking mixes—sourcing the best-quality ingredients (who knew biodynamic sugar even existed?) and developing the recipes to please us, since we were our target audience. We developed products that we were looking for (organic and ethically sourced anyone?), but could not find—baking mixes that feature the best, purest ingredients, each of them clearly listed on the package. Throughout this book you'll see recipes that call for boxed mixes. You can check out our current lines of mixes and kits at www.foodstirs.com and at select retail locations. Your recipe will still be easy as pie, and you'll have the peace of mind knowing that you're using the best ingredients possible.

Our mission is to make it easy and uncomplicated to gather in the kitchen and create something delicious, clever, and healthy to eat. Inspired by the DIY thread being pulled through all things culinary—just check out Pinterest and you will see what I mean—we sought to give home cooks a head start with our products.

But there is more to Foodstirs than the food. Our goal is to get at the emotional ties food forges, too. We like to think of our kits as courage in a box. Everything you need to make Pinterest-worthy baked goods is inside. We believe that whether you live next door to a natural grocery store or miles from your nearest neighbor, you should have access to premium-quality, affordable ingredients so that scratch baking becomes a daily joy. We like to think of Foodstirs as #HomeMadeEasy.

The best part of this book is that whether you are a novice or an expert, these recipes are for you.

And one last thought on cooking and ingredients: I know that choosing ingredients can be confusing these days, as there are so many healthy-sounding buzzwords like "natural" and "local." I like to choose my ingredients using the same philosophy with which I live my life: everything as fresh as possible, as unadulterated as possible, and made as close to home as possible. That's not to say I don't love a runny Camembert from France. What's more, while I love to indulge in a great sweet treat (or a savory one, for that matter), the main things I try to avoid are overprocessed foods and ingredients. I do not see a reason for using artificial colors when most colors can be extracted from plants (there are even dye-free sprinkles!). The only way I can be completely sure of what I am putting in my body (and my family's bodies) is to prepare our food myself—or more precisely, prepare it together with family and friends. It's the ideal group activity.

With the same spirit that I approached Foodstirs, Gia Russo, my friend, business partner, and coauthor, approached *Stirring Up Fun with Food*. We both have children—I have my daughter, Charlotte, and son, Rocky, and Gia has her son, Grayden. As soon as the kids could stand on a stepstool to reach the counters in our respective kitchens, we involved them in cooking. Of course, there is nothing like a kid to turn almost any activity into child's play, and that's when it occurred to us that playing with our food was not only fun, but mandatory! Making an apple pie is always fun, but putting a bite of it on a stick (page 224) is so much *more* fun! Making their dads cards for Father's Day is a big deal, but spelling out

The recipes that follow are <u>not</u> just for kids. In fact, we've tested every single one of them on adults.

what they want to say in fruit (page 138) makes the entire act of making, presenting, and receiving so much more thrilling. As mothers of school-age kids, we have packed dozens and dozens of lunches and understand the challenge of keeping it interesting. Threading almost anything onto a skewer does the trick; one of our favorite five-minute gourmet lunches is tortellini threaded onto a skewer (page 194) and served with a simple tomato dipping sauce.

In the following twelve chapters, organized by month, we've devised food for holidays, celebrations, and seasonal gatherings that is meant to add flair and excitement not only to your table, but to the preparation that happens beforehand.

Making it fun to make food is what we're after. If you own muffin tins, skewers, toothpicks, cookie cutters, mason jars, and juice glasses, you're halfway there. These are our go-to vessels and tools for making familiar dishes more interesting to prepare and to eat. We've witnessed how simply presenting a particular food in a fresh way can turn a "No way!" into a "Yes, please." If you slide a Caesar salad on a stick (yes, on a stick—check out page 169), there is a 100 percent greater chance that even the pickiest eater will go for it.

But the recipes that follow are not just for kids. In fact, we've tested every single one of them on adults. And it turns out that dads are just as intrigued by a Father's Day grilled cheese sandwich shaped like a tie (page 139) as the kids are entertained by making it. Young cooks love to make Mom a bouquet of flowers cut from vegetables (page 119) as much as she enjoys eating it. But it is perhaps the miniature cherry pies (page 51) that best exemplify what we have come to call food crafting. Baked in mason jar lids, they are easy to pop out of their molds once cooled. Why bake a pie in a pie tin when you could bake a much more charming version in a jar lid?

Our hope is that you will use the recipes on the following pages as inspiration, as a jumping-off point for coming up with your own clever food crafting ideas. So pull out your jars and ramekins, skewers and mini-muffin tins, and get crafting. You will likely find your time in the kitchen more joyful, nourishing, and satisfying than ever before.

French Onion Soup

Flavored Fruit &
Veggie Waters

Quiche Cupcakes

Fun-Shaped Egg-in-a-hole

PB&J Smoothie

JANUARY

Waffle Fondue

Truffle Mac 'n' Cheese "Cupcakes"

DIY Cookie-Decorating Bar

Vanilla Buttercream

Blackberry Yogurt Mask

I will never forget

ringing in the New Year in Australia in 1999. There was so much Y2K buzz in the air that I promised myself I would watch every celebration across the globe that night, since Australia would be the first country to see the clock strike twelve. Well, by the time New Year's hit Spain, I had fallen asleep!

The month itself carries with it so much promise. January gives us permission to press the reset button, to reevaluate and reshuffle priorities and maintain the rituals that bring us joy. Cooking dinner has always fallen into that last category. This is the month for an open house; on New Year's Day, we love to put together a menu that's festive and restorative. By throwing open the doors, we start the year off with the friends—new and old—and family who have long sustained us.

January is slumber party month in our respective homes—our kids always seem to want to hunker down with their friends and watch endless movies, giggle through the night, and of course, eat. We've found that kids have the most fun preparing the food they're going to eat (and put on their faces, as in the Blackberry Yogurt Mask, page 27) and even more so when their smoothies, waffles, and mac 'n' cheese are presented in unexpected ways.

We know all about resolutions and the earnestness with which we devise them. Preparing food with a bit of thought is a low-demand start. Marking the start of the year by slipping a delicious bite of waffle onto a stick or making mini quiches in a muffin tin, for example, gets you off on the right foot, food crafting–wise.

I rarely saw much of New Year's Day morning in my twenties. Back then, the holiday was all about the night before, with glitzy parties that stretched into the wee hours. Now I want nothing more than to wake up early, get the coffee going, and catch a few moments of solitude before the kids charge into the kitchen, raring to get breakfast started. The day is the culmination of what always turns out to be a crazy holiday season—and after so many party trays and pretty cocktails, rich desserts and extravagant entrées, all we really want is food that comforts, flavors that are familiar, and loving family and friends to share it all with.

All revelry from the night before will mellow with the first bite of this restorative comfort food. So simple to pull together, it features just six ingredients, most of which you probably have on hand. And forget the traditional crocks—just pull out a set of mason jars (they're ovenproof)!

Serves 8

French Onion soup

- 2 tablespoons olive oil, plus more for drizzling
- 3 large yellow onions, cut into ⅛-inch-thick slices
- 2 tablespoons fresh thyme, minced, plus additional sprigs for garnish
- 1 teaspoon kosher salt
- ½ teaspoon black pepper
- 6 cups beef stock or low-sodium beef broth
- 1 baguette, cut into ½-inch-thick slices
- 8 ounces Gruyère cheese, grated

In a large pot, heat the olive oil over medium heat. Add the onions and sauté until translucent, about 15 minutes. Add the thyme, salt, and pepper and sauté until fragrant, then add the stock. Bring to a boil, reduce the heat to low, cover, and simmer for 30 minutes.

Meanwhile, preheat the oven to 375°F. Place the baguette slices on a baking sheet and drizzle them all over with olive oil. Bake until golden, 8 to 10 minutes.

Ladle the soup into 12-ounce mason jars to within 1 inch from the rims, then add a few pieces of baguette. Sprinkle the cheese over the soup, dividing it evenly among the jars. Arrange the jars in a high-sided roasting pan and fill the pan with ½ inch of water. Bake until the cheese starts to bubble, 5 to 6 minutes. Garnish each jar with a few sprigs of thyme and serve hot, with a napkin wrapped around each jar (they will be hot to the touch).

Slaying thirst is essential on New Year's Day, and ideally you will choose lots of water with which to do it! But what could be less inspired than filling your cup straight from the tap? With the addition of fruits, vegetables, and herbs, a plain glass of water goes gourmet.

Makes 2 cups

FLAVORED Fruit & Veggie WATERS

Pineapple Mint Water

2 cups water or sparkling water

2 (½-inch-thick) slices pineapple, cut into quarters

¼ cup fresh mint leaves

Combine the water, pineapple, and mint in a pitcher and refrigerate for at least 1 hour and up to 4 hours to allow the flavors to develop. Serve cold. Garnish each glass with a pineapple slice and some mint from the pitcher.

Kiwi Cucumber Lime Water

2 cups water or sparkling water

2 kiwis, peeled and sliced into ¼-inch-thick slices

1 lime, thinly sliced

12 thin slices English cucumber

Combine the water, kiwis, limes, and cucumber in a pitcher and refrigerate for at least 1 hour and up to 4 hours to allow the flavors to develop. Serve cold. Garnish each glass with a kiwi, lime, and cucumber slice from the pitcher.

Blackberry Water

1 cup blackberries

2 cups water or sparkling water

½ orange, cut into quarters

Put half the blackberries in a pitcher. Using the back of a spoon, gently mash them. (This not only releases a bit of their juice, but tints the water a gorgeous pink.).

Add the remaining whole blackberries, the water, and the orange and refrigerate for at least 1 hour and up to 4 hours to allow the flavors to develop. Serve cold. Garnish each glass with some blackberries and orange from the pitcher.

A wedge is nice, but a personal petite quiche has a lot going for it, not least the impression that you took the time to prepare something special.

Makes 24 cupcakes

Quiche
CUPCAKES

- 2 (14.1-ounce) packages prepared piecrust rounds
- 3 ounces pancetta, diced
- 4 ounces Gruyère cheese, grated
- 8 large eggs
- 1⅓ cups milk or heavy cream
- 2 teaspoons finely chopped flat-leaf parsley, plus more for garnish

  Black pepper

Preheat the oven to 350°F. Coat two 12-cup muffin tins with cooking spray.

On a lightly floured surface, roll each piecrust round out to about 10 inches. Using a 3½-inch round cutter or an overturned cup or jar, cut out several rounds from each crust. Press the dough scraps together, roll out again, and cut several more rounds. Repeat until you have 24 rounds. Place a round into each cup of the prepared muffin tins, pressing them into the seams with your fingers to form cups. Put 1 teaspoon of the pancetta and 2 tablespoons of the cheese into each crust.

In a large bowl, whisk together the eggs, milk, and parsley. Divide the egg mixture among the muffin cups; the liquid should almost reach the rim of each cup. Sprinkle pepper on each and bake until the crust is golden and the eggs are set, about 25 minutes. When cool enough to handle, remove the quiches from the tins. Serve at room temperature, garnished with additional parsley.

There's nothing quite like the beautiful simplicity of an egg on toast. It's an apt way to launch into the New Year, especially if it's made with a little more care and attention than your standard version. With nothing more than a cookie cutter (maybe they are still hanging around from all of that holiday baking?), the classic breakfast becomes a sunny way to start the day.

This recipe can be doubled, tripled, quadrupled—scaled up to feed everyone in the house.

Makes 1 serving

FUN-SHAPED
Egg-in-a Hole

1 slice of your favorite bread, preferably a Pullman or other variety with a dense crumb

1 large egg

1 tablespoon unsalted butter, plus softened butter for serving

Kosher salt and black pepper

Use a cookie cutter of about 2 inches in diameter to cut out the center of the bread. Toast the cut-out center in the toaster; set the bread slice aside.

Crack the egg into a small bowl. In a skillet, melt the butter over medium-low heat. Place the bread slice in the pan and pour the egg into the center. Season the egg with salt and pepper and cook until the yolk begins to turn opaque, about 1 minute. Using a large spatula, flip the bread over and fry until the bread is golden and the yolk is cooked to your liking, about 1 minute more for over-easy. Serve immediately, with the toasted cutout and softened butter for spreading.

Clever presentation is A LOT EASIER than it looks.

slumber PARTY

Slumber means sleep, but that's not necessarily what goes on at a sleepover, if our experiences are any indication. So we focus on what we can control, which is how much fun it can be to get kids into the kitchen to make the food they're going to eat. And they *will* eat. Gia's son has become famous among his friends for his PB&J smoothie, in fact. At my house, the entertainment largely takes place in the kitchen rather than in front of a screen; from whirring up yummy juices, to decorating cookies, to making mac 'n' cheese perfumed with truffle oil. My daughter can never seem to wait for the breakfast waffles on a stick, which is fine by me. They're even okay for dinner every once in a while!

A no-brainer for the slumber set
(it's also a great pre-practice boost for the athletes
in your house), this concoction is a healthy
alternative to a sugary shake. Set out the ingredients
and invite the pajama party to participate.

**Makes one 16-ounce
or two 8-ounce smoothies**

PB&J smoothie

1 cup frozen blueberries

1 banana

½ cup plain Greek yogurt

2 tablespoons peanut butter

1 tablespoon honey

Combine all the ingredients in a blender and blend until smooth, about 1 minute. If the smoothie is too thick to pour, add water 1 tablespoon at a time with the blender running until the texture is to your liking. Serve immediately in a simple clear glass jar with a colorful straw (or two).

Waffle FONDUE

We devised this presentation for our kids' favorite breakfast treat out of cunning, truthfully. When it came time to clear the breakfast dishes, each one had a puddle of maple syrup left behind; let's just say that it's fun to pour *tons* of syrup onto waffles. Our solution? Treat them like crudités, with waffle bites on toothpicks and tiny cups, bowls, and vessels of syrup for dipping.

The syrups will keep, covered tightly and refrigerated, up to one week.

Serves 6 to 8

8 to 10 frozen Belgian waffles, toasted and cut into quarters

Honey-Peach Syrup (recipe follows)

Vanilla Bean Maple Syrup (recipe follows)

Fresh Berry Maple Syrup (recipe follows)

Using decorative toothpicks, pierce each waffle piece and arrange several on a plate with individual servings of each syrup for dipping.

Honey-Peach Syrup

¾ cup honey

½ cup peach fruit spread, such as Bonne Maman

Pinch of kosher salt

Combine the honey, fruit spread, salt, and 2 tablespoons water in a medium saucepan. Cook over medium heat, stirring often, until loose and smooth. Let cool slightly before serving.

Makes about 1¼ cups

Vanilla Bean Maple Syrup

2 cups maple syrup

1 (6-inch) vanilla bean, split lengthwise and seeds scraped

Combine the maple syrup, vanilla bean pod, and vanilla seeds in a medium saucepan. Bring to a simmer over medium heat and cook for 5 minutes. Remove from the heat and discard the bean pod. Let cool slightly before serving.

Makes 2 cups

Fresh Berry Maple Syrup

1 cup maple syrup

1 cup coarsely chopped fresh blackberries or hulled strawberries

Combine the maple syrup and berries in a medium saucepan. Bring to a simmer over medium heat and cook, stirring occasionally, for 5 minutes. Let cool slightly before serving.

Makes 1½ to 2 cups

Dip! Don't DROWN waffles in maple syrup.

TRUFFLE Mac 'n' Cheese "CUPCAKES"

We know there are some seemingly healthy packaged mac 'n' cheese options at the grocery store, but they seem like fuel rather than food because they come together so fast. Which is the point. But with ever-so-slightly more effort, you can fill your kitchen with the unmistakable fragrance of burbling macaroni and cheese, an aroma that will draw your grown children back home long after they've built lives of their own. These make wonderful, filling snacks, lunches, light dinners, or hors d'oeuvres.

Makes 24 "cupcakes"

5 tablespoons unsalted butter

½ cup grated Parmesan cheese

1 pound elbow macaroni

1 tablespoon truffle oil (optional)

1½ teaspoons black pepper

1 teaspoon kosher salt

1 teaspoon Dijon mustard

½ teaspoon garlic powder

½ teaspoon paprika

2 tablespoons all-purpose flour

2 cups milk

1 cup half-and-half

1½ cups shredded sharp white cheddar cheese

1 cup shredded mild cheddar cheese

¾ cup shredded Fontina cheese

½ cup shredded Gruyère cheese

Preheat the oven to 375°F. Melt 1 tablespoon of the butter and use it to coat two 12-cup muffin tins. Dust the wells with the Parmesan, shaking out any excess.

Bring a large pot of water to a boil. Add the macaroni and cook according to the package instructions. Drain and transfer to a large bowl. Add the truffle oil (if using) and toss to coat. Set aside.

In a large saucepan, melt the remaining 4 tablespoons of butter over medium heat. Add the pepper, salt, mustard, garlic powder, and paprika and whisk until combined. Gradually add the flour, whisking continuously to prevent clumping. Cook until the mixture begins to bubble. While whisking, slowly pour in the milk and half-and-half. Return the mixture to a boil and remove from the heat. Add the cheeses and whisk vigorously until all the cheese has melted and the sauce is smooth.

Pour the cheese sauce over the macaroni and stir until thoroughly coated. Divide the mac 'n' cheese evenly among the prepared muffin cups and bake for 15 to 20 minutes, or until the tops of the cupcakes are browned and bubbling. Let the cupcakes set for 10 minutes before removing them from the tins. Serve warm.

DIY Cookie-DECORATING Bar

Messy, charming, festive—these are the ingredients of a successful kids' party, and we've found that decorating cookies includes all three. There's something for everyone—some kids focus on color combinations, others are drawn to designs and the decorations, while still others love to use the piping bag. To save time, purchase the cookies and make just the buttercream frosting. Divide it among bowls and color with food coloring. Spoon it into several piping bags fitted with different tips and set them in tall glasses to hold. Dispense decorations—sprinkles and sparkling sugars—in small bowls and arrange cookies on a large platter. It's a party!

RECIPE continues

Continued

This universally loved and easy-to-spread frosting can be made a day in advance. Store it tightly covered in the refrigerator and bring to room temperature before using.

Makes about 3 cups

VANILLA Buttercream

1 cup (2 sticks) unsalted butter, at room temperature

4 cups confectioners' sugar

¼ cup heavy cream

½ teaspoon kosher salt

In a large bowl, use an electric mixer to cream the butter. Add the sugar, cream, and salt and beat until the mixture is smooth and fluffy, about 5 minutes.

What could be more fun for a gaggle of kids than slathering a cool, creamy potion all over one another's faces? This mask contains nothing but ingredients you would gladly put *in* your body, which is a good message to impart to your children. Blackberries are packed with antioxidants, and both yogurt and coconut oil are super hydrating—but more important, the combination is good enough to eat!

Makes enough for 4 applications

BLACKBERRY Yogurt Mask

¼ cup plain Greek yogurt
2 tablespoons honey
⅓ cup fresh blackberries
2 teaspoons coconut oil

Combine all the ingredients in a food processor or blender and pulse until smooth. Immediately apply to clean skin and leave on for 10 to 20 minutes. Rinse away with warm water. The mixture can be made in advance, covered tightly, and refrigerated for up to 5 days.

Roasted Tomato Soup
with Grilled Cheese Dippers

Meatloaf Muffins

TV Turkey Chili

Cauliflower Popcorn

FEBRUARY

Chocolate X & O
Truffle Cupcakes

Chocolate Mousse Pudding

Strawberry & Watermelon
Hearts

Not surprisingly,

we favor food-centric holidays and celebrations over any other, which is why February is so appealing. Unlike those celebrations that call for decorations and gifts (not counting giving actual Valentines, which, to my dismay, turns out to be a competitive sport among my kids' classmates!), the gatherings this month revolve around comfort and indulgence, which makes sense. The gleam of the holidays has dulled and the chill of winter has set in.

It's time to get cozy on the sofa and tuck into food that instantly warms and nourishes: hearty chili, piping-hot soup, succulent meat loaf. We've devised versions of each of these for Super Bowl Sunday, each one presented in a way that makes it easy to jump up off the couch for the big score without tossing food in the air. And then there's our "popcorn," tiny cauliflower florets tossed with seasonings that is as addictive as any movie version. This is not plate-in-your-lap, fork-in-hand-style food—who has time to fiddle when there's football to watch?

Indeed, we're intent on taking the traditional formality—and expected approach—out of preparing delicious food. Especially when it comes to Valentine's Day. It's funny—I've never been much of a traditionalist when it comes to this holiday. So when it came to creating a menu for Valentine's Day, we went straight to chocolate, naturally, along with our favorite red fruits, and then used nothing more than a muffin tin, mason jar lids, a cookie cutter, and tiny glasses to change up the presentation of truffles, mousse, and even pie (baked in the lids!). But don't wait until February 14 to make these recipes; everyone loves a sweet, especially when it is sweetly conceived.

Super Bowl

I was at the 1999 Super Bowl—the
Denver Broncos beat the Atlanta Falcons by 15 points.
After that, I realized just how much better the view—
and the food—is from the sofa!

We've skipped the wings and blue cheese dip,
the nachos and the heaping supermarket cold cuts in favor
of somewhat more healthful comforts. There's
no need to wait for game day to turn these out, however.
These can all be arranged on the coffee table and
guests can eat as they please.

ROASTED Tomato Soup WITH GRILLED Cheese DIPPERS

This beloved combination is delicious no matter how it's served, but when you pour it into a charming mix of little shot glasses and cut the sandwiches into strips perfectly sized for dipping, it becomes much more than a lunchtime classic.

Serves 8 to 12

RECIPE continues

Continued

FOR THE SOUP

6 garlic cloves

4 tablespoons olive oil, divided

4 pounds plum tomatoes, halved lengthwise

2 tablespoons fresh basil, minced

2 teaspoons fresh oregano

1 teaspoon fresh thyme, minced

Kosher salt and black pepper

3 cups vegetable broth

2 teaspoons sugar (optional)

FOR THE DIPPERS

6 tablespoons (¾ stick) butter, at room temperature

12 slices sourdough bread

6 ounces mild cheddar cheese, shredded

6 ounces mozzarella cheese, shredded

⅓ cup grated Parmesan cheese

TO MAKE THE SOUP: Preheat the oven to 425°F.

Place the garlic cloves on a piece of foil and drizzle with 1 tablespoon of the olive oil. Wrap the foil around the cloves and seal tightly. Place the tomatoes on a baking sheet. Sprinkle the tomatoes with the remaining 3 tablespoons of the olive oil, the basil, oregano, thyme, and salt and pepper to taste, then toss to coat. Place the garlic packet on the baking sheet with the tomatoes and roast until the tomatoes are soft and caramelized, about 30 minutes. Transfer the tomatoes and garlic to a food processor or a blender. Add the broth and process until smooth. Pour the mixture into a large soup pot and simmer over low heat until thoroughly heated, 25 to 30 minutes. Taste and adjust the seasonings, adding the sugar to balance the acidity, if desired. Keep the soup hot.

TO MAKE THE DIPPERS: Heat a griddle over medium heat. Butter one side of each slice of bread. Place a slice of bread on the griddle pan, buttered-side down, and top with 1 ounce each of the cheddar and mozzarella cheeses. Top with another slice of bread, buttered-side up. Once the cheese begins to melt and the bottom slice is crisp and golden, flip the sandwich using a spatula. Sprinkle the top with Parmesan. When the bottom slice is crisp and golden, flip the sandwich again and sprinkle the top with Parmesan. Repeat with the remaining bread and cheeses. Cut each sandwich into 4 to 6 strips and serve warm alongside the soup.

A DELIGHT
for the
tiniest
dippers.

One comfort food shaped like another! There's nothing like a slice of piping-hot meat loaf, except one that comes in a compact little package like this. They can practically be eaten out of one hand, a napkin in the other. Warm meat loaf is the best, but everyone knows how satisfying it can be to eat it cold when hunger strikes. We've both been known to keep this in the refrigerator for an easy after-school snack.

Makes 12 muffins

Meatloaf MUFFINS

2 tablespoons olive oil

1 large yellow onion, diced

1½ cups grated carrot

2 teaspoons minced garlic

Kosher salt and black pepper

2 teaspoons Worcestershire sauce

2 (6-ounce) cans tomato paste

2 cups seasoned bread crumbs

2 large eggs

1 egg white

2 pounds ground turkey or lean ground beef

Chopped fresh parsley, for garnish

Preheat the oven to 400°F. Coat the wells of a 12-cup muffin tin with cooking spray.

In a large skillet, heat the olive oil over medium heat. Add the onion, carrot, and garlic and cook until softened and fragrant, 8 to 10 minutes. Season with salt and pepper. Add the Worcestershire and 3 tablespoons of the tomato paste and stir until combined. Transfer the mixture to a large bowl.

Add the bread crumbs to the vegetable mixture and stir to combine. Add the eggs and ground turkey and, using your hands, mix until thoroughly incorporated. Divide the mixture into 12 equal balls, place one in each well of the prepared muffin tin, and press firmly so the turkey mixture fills the well. Spread the remaining tomato paste evenly over each muffin.

Bake until the meat loaves are cooked through, about 30 minutes. Let cool slightly, then remove from the tins by running a knife around the edges. Garnish with parsley and serve warm.

Mason jars are indispensable in our kitchens; they stand in for glassware, bowls, crocks—you name it. What's more, they're heatproof. Here, a warming chili—seasoned with cumin, chili powder, paprika, and cayenne—is spooned into the jars and served with a tray of choose-your-own toppings. It's ideal for a warm snack on a chilly winter afternoon, not to mention enjoying while sitting on the sofa.

Makes about 12 cups

3 tablespoons olive oil

3 garlic cloves, minced

1 large yellow onion, chopped

1 large bell pepper, coarsely chopped

1 pound ground turkey

3 tablespoons chili powder

1½ teaspoons kosher salt

1 tablespoon ground cumin

1 teaspoon Hungarian paprika

½ teaspoon cayenne pepper

1 teaspoon dried oregano

1 (28-ounce) can diced tomatoes

1 cup chicken stock or low-sodium chicken broth

1 (15-ounce) can black beans, drained and rinsed

1 (15-ounce) can kidney beans, drained and rinsed

OPTIONAL TOPPINGS

Shredded cheddar cheese

Tortilla chips

Limes, cut into eighths

Avocados, peeled and cut into chunks

Sour cream or plain Greek yogurt

Chopped fresh cilantro leaves

TV TURKEY Chili

In a large pot, heat the olive oil over medium heat. Add the garlic, onion, and bell pepper and cook until soft and fragrant, 8 to 10 minutes. Add the turkey and cook, breaking it up with a wooden spoon, until it loses its pink color, 3 to 5 minutes. Season with the chili powder, salt, cumin, paprika, cayenne, and oregano and stir until thoroughly incorporated. Add the tomatoes with their juices, broth, and beans and stir. Bring to a boil, then reduce the heat to medium low and simmer, uncovered, until the tomatoes break down, about 30 minutes.

Arrange the toppings of your choice in small bowls and set them on the table alongside the pot of chili and mason jars, buffet-style.

Gia grew up eating classic Italian preparations of cauliflower, but all of them required a fork. A big bowl of popcorn may be a Super Bowl staple, but we're positive this little bait and switch will become as much in demand from the first handful. Nutritional yeast, a vegan substitute for cheese, is generally available in the bulk foods section of most natural food stores. Not only is its nutty flavor addicting, but the flakes are loaded with B vitamins. If cheese or yeast doesn't appeal, use lemon zest, chopped rosemary, or curry powder.

Serves 12

CAULIFLOWER Popcorn

2 large heads cauliflower, halved and cored

3 tablespoons olive oil

1 teaspoon kosher salt

¼ cup grated Parmesan cheese or nutritional yeast

Preheat the oven to 425°F.

Break the cauliflower into popcorn-size pieces and put them in a large bowl. Add the olive oil and toss to coat. Season with the salt. Spread the cauliflower in a single layer on a rimmed baking sheet or two and roast until tender and golden, about 25 minutes. Let cool slightly, then sprinkle with the Parmesan. Transfer to a large serving bowl and pass with napkins.

For some, much rides on this saint's day; for others, it's a chance to remind a longtime love of how special he or she is. For me, it used to be a non-holiday. And I said so in a magazine interview when I was in my late teens. I very confidently suggested that I was anti-Valentine's Day, that it should be a day for everyone, with partners or without. I said something about how much more romantic it is to be surprised by flowers or chocolate, to be presented with them out of the blue. Apparently, Fred Savage read the article, and sent me flowers as a result. I had not known him before this, but we have remained friends ever since! I'll always fall for chocolates, but instead of a clichéd heart-shaped box, I'd rather give (or receive!) homemade chocolate truffle cupcakes or chocolate mousse. Food crafting is all about charm and ease, and nowhere is that better embodied than in the tiny cherry pies in this section—they're baked in mason jar lids.

CHOCOLATE X & O TRUFFLE cupcakes

Sometimes a hug and a kiss are all it takes. Gia and her son make these for him to hand out to his class instead of paper Valentines. You'll note that we call for a boxed cake mix, because let's face it, sometimes time doesn't allow for a full from-scratch version, especially if you're one ingredient short and can't run out to the grocery store. Look for the best-quality mix you can find, such as Foodstirs. And keep in mind that you will need a few additional ingredients (eggs, for example) when using one. Where confectioners' sugar is typically tapped all over a chocolate cake like a light snowfall, we took the opportunity to say something with it instead. By using an old-school stencil, found in the school supply aisle at the art supply store or at a stationery shop, you can say whatever you want. The simplest (and sweetest) is an *X* and *O*, two letters that are worth a thousand words. Be sure to let the cupcakes cool a bit before decorating them.

Makes 24 cupcakes

RECIPE continues

Continued

½ cup heavy cream

8 ounces good-quality dark chocolate, finely chopped

¼ teaspoon pure vanilla extract

1 (15.25-ounce) box chocolate cake mix

½ cup confectioners' sugar

In a small saucepan, heat the cream over medium heat until just before it starts to boil. Remove from the heat immediately and let cool slightly. Add the chocolate to the pan and whisk continuously until it melts and the mixture is smooth. Stir in the vanilla. Set aside for 1 hour; it will firm up.

Line a baking sheet with parchment paper. Using a teaspoon, scoop rounded spoonfuls of the chocolate mixture onto the baking sheet. Refrigerate until firm, about 45 minutes. Remove the truffles from the refrigerator and, using your hands, roll each chocolate mound into a ball. Return the truffles to the baking sheet and freeze for at least 1 hour.

Meanwhile, line two 12-cup muffin tins with festive paper liners. Prepare the cake batter according to the package directions. Fill each well of the muffin tins two-thirds full with batter, then place a chocolate truffle in the center of the batter in each, pushing it down into the batter so the chocolate is covered entirely. Bake according to the package directions. Let the cupcakes cool. Position a stencil over a cupcake and use a sieve to tap confectioners' sugar over the top. Carefully remove the stencil and repeat with the remaining cupcakes.

With the simple addition of a heart-shaped strawberry set on top, this unassuming—yet delicious—mousse becomes a perfect treat for a sweetheart.

Makes 3 cups

Chocolate Mousse PUDDING

2 cups heavy cream

½ cup granulated sugar

1 (4-ounce) package instant chocolate pudding mix

1 tablespoon unsweetened cocoa powder

Strawberry Hearts (page 48)

Confectioners' sugar, for dusting

In a large bowl, use an electric mixer to whip the cream on medium-high speed. As the cream begins to thicken, gradually add the granulated sugar and whip until soft peaks form. Reduce the mixer speed to medium-low, add the pudding mix and cocoa powder, and mix until thoroughly incorporated.

Spoon the pudding into shot glasses. (Alternatively, spoon it into a piping bag fitted with a decorative tip of your choice and pipe the pudding into the shot glasses.) Refrigerate for at least 2 hours. Top each with a Strawberry Heart and serve on a platter dusted with confectioners' sugar.

When Gia was a stylist at *Martha Stewart Living*, she was often preparing stories for the February issue in late summer, which is the inspiration behind this combination. Now that you can get watermelon and strawberries year-round, this duo is a sweet way to treat your Valentine and keep it healthy at the same time. Slip the hearts on skewers and tuck them into a pretty glass.

Makes 8 skewers

STRAWBERRY & WATERMELON hearts

1 pint whole strawberries, halved lengthwise

½ seedless watermelon

Using a sharp paring knife, cut the stems out of the strawberries in a V-shape. Cut the watermelon into 1-inch-thick slices. Using a 1½-inch heart-shaped cookie cutter, cut out hearts from the watermelon slices. Thread the hearts onto 8-inch skewers in the desired order. Serve in a clear glass.

Two-part mason jar lids are like mini springform pans without the spring. You can bake two-bite pies in them and easily remove the "ring" for serving. These make use of the ready-made piecrusts you can find in the freezer section of the grocery store, which can fool even the most die-hard home baker!

PALM-SIZE Cherry pies

Makes 6

1½ cups fresh cherries, pitted

¼ cup plus 1 tablespoon sugar

1 tablespoon all-purpose flour

1 refrigerated rolled piecrust

1 egg yolk

Preheat the oven to 375°F. Arrange six mason jar rings fitted with lids on a baking sheet.

Combine the cherries, ¼ cup of the sugar, and ¼ cup water in a medium saucepan and bring to a boil. Reduce the heat, stir in the flour, and simmer until the mixture thickens slightly, 5 to 10 minutes. Set aside to cool.

Place the piecrust on a clean work surface and cut out 6 rounds, each about 1 inch larger in diameter than the mason jar rings. Wrap the leftover dough in plastic wrap and refrigerate. Place one round in each mason jar ring, scalloping the edges with your index finger and thumb. Using a fork, prick holes all over the bottom of each crust. Bake until lightly golden, about 10 minutes.

Meanwhile, roll out the reserved dough scraps to ¼-inch thickness. Using a 1½-inch heart-shaped cookie cutter, a very sharp knife, or an X-ACTO knife, cut out heart shapes.

Fill the crusts evenly with the cherry mixture and place a heart cutout on top. Whisk together the egg yolk and 1 tablespoon water with a fork and brush this egg wash over the crusts and hearts. Sprinkle with the remaining sugar and bake until the filling is bubbling, about 10 minutes. Let cool slightly.

Run a sharp knife around the ring to loosen the crust. Pop out, remove bottom and serve.

Veggie Egg Rolls

Skewered Dumplings

Blood Orange with
Crystallized Ginger

Shrimp Lomein "Cupcakes"

MARCH

Chilled Avocado Soup

Edamame Hummus &
Shamrock Pita

Green Eggs & Ham Pinch Pots

Green Fruit on a Stick

In the Prince household,

March is a big month. For Freddie, it's the celebration of his birth and for me, it's the celebration of spring cleaning (yes, I am that person).

Growing up in New York City, one of the first adventurous foods I ate was Chinese take-out, which led to my life-long interest in Chinese culture. They believe in the art (yes, I said "art") of spring cleaning. The tradition is to not just clean and reorganize the home, but to make noise to scare away bad spirits, and then feast with family and friends. So, once I have used my broom to "sweep" out the old, it's time to eat. There is nothing like making dumplings and egg rolls to get anyone hooked on the magic of making your own food. And, if the takeout variety is all you have known, the act of pressing dumplings and folding egg roll wrappers makes an even greater impression (Note: you do not need to clean your house to appreciate these delicacies.)

March is also the month St. Patrick's Day is in, so why not take this opportunity to push as much green food as possible? My kids have been eating vegetables since they were old enough to swallow (pureed, of course, before they cut their teeth!) and, as a result, the vegetables on their plate are the first to go. So we skipped the traditional corned beef and cabbage and instead took inspiration from the color associated with Ireland. What better reason to go heavy on green vegetables and ignore green food coloring? The only green in our Green Eggs and Ham (page 70) is nutrient-loaded spinach. There's no artificial color that comes close to the gorgeous green of the pureed avocados in a chilled soup or of edamame hummus that can be scooped up with shamrock-shaped toasted pita. Of course, green food is good food any time of year; why not prepare these dishes year-round?

Better Than Take-Out

As I mentioned, I have always been fascinated by Chinese culture. I may not know a lot about Western astrological signs, but I am a Chinese zodiac expert. Freddie was born in the "year of the dragon" (and he has the tattoo to prove it), and I was born in the "year of the snake." Interestingly, the attributes and the sayings of each are a perfect match. The dragon represents strength while the snake represents flexibility. Traditionally the sayings are: "Strength without flexibility leads to fracture" and "flexibility without strength leads to compromise." It sounds like we were made for each other. Equally, we were made to love Chinese cooking.

While dumplings and egg rolls may seem like obvious choices, blood oranges may not. In Chinese, the word *orange* sounds very similar to the word for wealth, so an orange is often associated with prosperity. And, really, who am I to argue with such a lucky fruit?

VEGGIE egg rolls

Gia's son is obsessed with Chinese food. She thinks it's because when she was carrying him, she ordered in chicken with broccoli and dumplings at least three times a week. Needless to say, these are among his favorite things to make.

Egg rolls may appear to be a bit involved, but with a few pairs of helping hands—my kids love to use the grater and measuring cups and spoons—you can turn the preparation time into a festivity in and of itself. Making them has become a ritual in both of our kitchens, and a welcome one at that; everyone gets into the act and we eat casually, as the egg rolls come out of the pan.

Makes about 12 egg rolls

RECIPE continues

Continued

2 teaspoons sesame oil

3 scallions, green parts cut into 1½-inch strips and white parts finely chopped

1 tablespoon minced fresh ginger

1 tablespoon minced garlic

1½ cups shredded cabbage

8 shiitake mushrooms, cut into 1½-inch matchsticks

1 cup bean sprouts

1 large carrot, cut into 1½-inch matchsticks

1 teaspoon sugar

1 tablespoon soy sauce

1 teaspoon white pepper

1 egg white

12 square spring roll wrappers

Canola oil, for frying

Plum sauce, for serving (optional)

Heat the sesame oil in a large skillet over medium heat. Add the scallion whites, ginger, and garlic and sauté until the scallions soften, about 3 minutes. Add the cabbage, mushrooms, sprouts, and carrots and sprinkle in the sugar. Cook until the vegetables begin to soften, then season with the soy sauce and white pepper. Cook until the soy sauce has evaporated, then remove from heat. Toss in the scallion greens and stir to combine thoroughly. Set the mixture aside to cool completely before filling.

Meanwhile, whisk together the egg white and 1 tablespoon water in a small bowl.

Place a spring roll wrapper on a work surface with a corner facing you. In the lower third of the wrapper, place a small spoonful of the vegetable filling, leaving ¼ inch of dough around it. Fold the lower corner over the filling and begin to tightly roll the wrapper, lightly brushing the exposed wrapper with the egg white mixture as you roll and folding in the two side corners as you go. Repeat with remaining egg rolls and filling. Cover tightly with plastic wrap and refrigerate until ready to cook.

Fill a skillet with ½ inch of canola oil and heat over medium-high heat. The oil is hot enough when a drop of water spatters when it hits the oil. Place a few egg rolls in the pan, being careful not to crowd the pan, and fry until golden, turning frequently, about 5 minutes. Using a slotted spoon, transfer the egg rolls to a paper towel–lined plate. Repeat with the remaining rolls. Serve warm with soy sauce or plum sauce for dipping, if desired.

Eating anything bound up in a tiny bundle is inherently fun, but when you also get to pick it up with your hands—by way of a stick—it's even more so. Of course, these are traditionally eaten with chopsticks, but a better way to introduce them to tiny hands might be to serve them this way; there's a lot less fumbling, and a lot more of the package lands in their mouths! Kids also love their own little bowl of dipping sauce. (By the way, I use this presentation for waffles, too, because it cuts back on the sugar consumption!)

SKEWERED dumplings

Makes 36 dumplings

12 ounces ground chicken

2 scallions, finely chopped

½ cup shredded cabbage

1½ teaspoons minced fresh ginger

¾ teaspoon minced garlic

3 tablespoons low-sodium soy sauce plus more for serving

½ teaspoon chili oil or sesame oil

1 package round wonton skins

1 egg white, lightly beaten

3 to 4 tablespoons canola oil

Combine the chicken, scallions, cabbage, ginger, and garlic in a large bowl and mix with a wooden spoon or with your hands until well combined. Add the soy sauce and chili oil and mix until thoroughly coated. Place a wonton wrapper on a clean work surface. Spoon about 1 teaspoon of the chicken filling into the center of the wrapper. Lightly brush the edges of the wrapper with the egg white, then fold it in half, crimping the edges with a fork to seal. Set the filled dumpling on a plate and repeat with the remaining wrappers and filling. Cover with plastic wrap and refrigerate until ready to cook. The dumplings can be made up to a few hours in advance.

Pour ½ cup water into a large nonstick skillet with a lid and place over medium heat. Place several dumplings in the pan, making sure they don't touch. Cover and steam for about 4 minutes. Transfer to a plate with a slotted spoon. Once all the dumplings have been steamed, pour out the water from the pan, wipe out the pan with a paper towel, and heat 2 tablespoons of canola oil over medium-high heat. Working in batches, place the dumplings in the pan, sealed edges up, and fry until golden, 2 to 3 minutes, adjusting the heat to keep them from burning. Slip one or two dumplings onto a skewer (see photo on page 62) and serve with soy sauce for dipping.

We make these cooling little cups of sweet oranges tinged with the pleasant bite of ginger as much as possible during blood orange season. They're not only gorgeous, but the perfect ending to *any* meal.

Serves 6

blood Orange with CRYSTALLIZED GINGER

3 navel or blood oranges, ends trimmed

1 tablespoon sugar

1 tablespoon crystallized ginger

Cut the oranges in half crosswise. Take one orange half and run a knife between the flesh and the rind, cutting right through the bottom. Remove the flesh from the rind, keeping the halves intact, and set aside. Repeat with the remaining orange halves.

Separate the orange flesh into segments by cutting along the sides of the membranes. Return the segments to the orange halves.

Sprinkle each orange cup with ½ teaspoon each of the sugar and crystallized ginger. Place in bowls or on a platter, wrap in plastic, and refrigerate until ready to serve.

Shrimp Lomein "Cupcakes" in bowl and
Skewered Dumplings (see page 59).

Noodles baked into nests make excellent "bowls" for holding all manner of fillings—here they become a deconstructed lo mein that can be eaten out of your hand. It's a clever spin on that classic takeout dish. Feel free to swap out the shrimp for rotisserie chicken, tofu, or diced ham. These make excellent after-school snacks and are delicious both warm and at room temperature.

Makes 24 "cupcakes"

shrimp lo mein "CUPCAKES"

1 pound lo mein noodles

2 large eggs, lightly beaten

½ cup plus 2 tablespoons teriyaki sauce

1 tablespoon toasted sesame seeds

1 tablespoon toasted sesame oil

1 tablespoon vegetable oil

1 cup matchstick-cut carrots

¾ cup thinly sliced red onion

¾ cup chopped red bell pepper

3 cups thinly sliced green cabbage

2 garlic cloves, finely chopped

2 teaspoons finely grated fresh ginger

¾ pound medium shrimp (about 24), peeled and deveined

3 tablespoons chopped fresh cilantro

Kosher salt and black pepper

Preheat the oven to 350°F. Lightly grease two 12-cup muffin tins with canola oil and line them with 5-inch squares of parchment paper or paper cupcake liners.

Bring a pot of water to a boil. Add the noodles and cook until just slightly undercooked, about 2 minutes. Drain and rinse under cool water. In a small bowl, whisk together the eggs, ½ cup of the teriyaki sauce, and the sesame seeds. Pour the egg mixture over the noodles and toss to coat.

Divide the noodle mixture among the prepared muffin cups. Using the back of a spoon, make a slight indentation in the center of the noodles. Bake until set, about 20 minutes.

Meanwhile, heat the sesame and vegetable oils in a large nonstick skillet over high heat. Add the carrots, onion, and bell pepper and sauté for 1 minute. Stir in the cabbage, garlic, and ginger and cook until fragrant, about 1 minute. Stir in the shrimp and cook until the edges become opaque, about 1 minute. Stir in the remaining 2 tablespoons teriyaki sauce and cook until the shrimp are entirely opaque, about 1 minute more. Remove from the heat and fold in the cilantro. Season with salt and black pepper. Divide the vegetable-shrimp mixture among the muffin cups and serve warm.

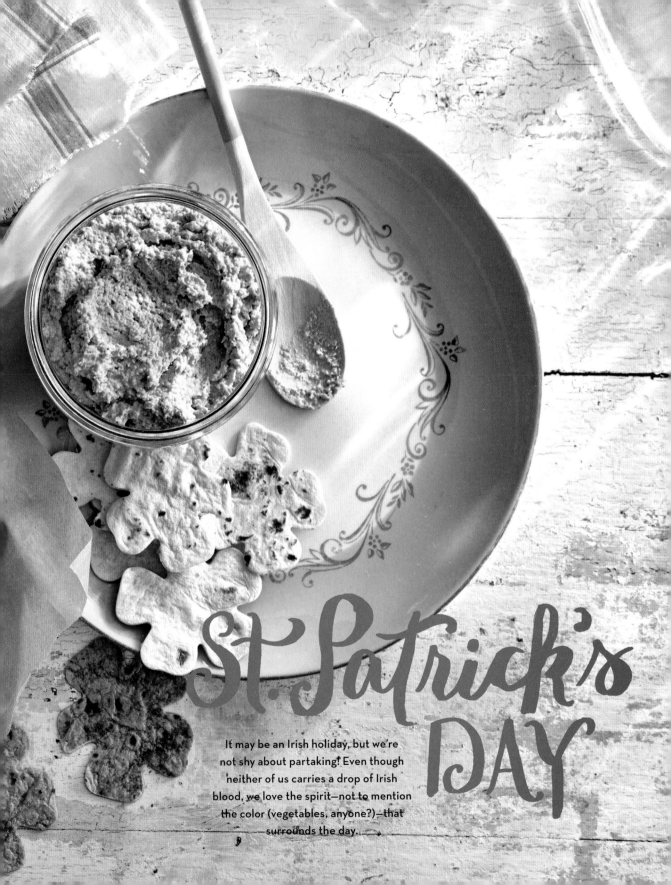

St. Patrick's DAY

It may be an Irish holiday, but we're not shy about partaking! Even though neither of us carries a drop of Irish blood, we love the spirit—not to mention the color (vegetables, anyone?)—that surrounds the day.

When you live in Southern California like we do, avocados are a staple. Simple, delicious, and beautiful, this lovely soup takes full advantage of the bounty. It looks as good as it tastes, so serve it in clear glass vessels. Jam jars work nicely, as do Weck jars or drinking glasses.

Makes 4 cups

CHILLED Avocado Soup

4 Hass avocados

3 cups vegetable broth

¼ cup fresh cilantro, plus more for garnish

2 tablespoons fresh lemon juice

1 tablespoon fresh lime juice

¾ teaspoon white pepper

½ teaspoon kosher salt

Lime wedges, for garnish

Peel the avocados and cut them into large chunks. Place the avocados, broth, cilantro, lemon juice, lime juice, pepper, and salt in a food processor or blender and process until smooth. Taste and adjust the seasonings as needed. Pour the soup into a large glass pitcher and refrigerate until chilled. Pour the soup into glass vessels and garnish with lime wedges and cilantro.

By using edamame in place of chickpeas and simply cutting pita into shamrock shapes, you can turn a classic hors d'oeuvre into a holiday treat.

Makes about 3 cups hummus

Edamame hummus & SHAMROCK PITA

3 cups cooked shelled edamame
¼ cup tahini
3 garlic cloves
Juice of 1 lemon
1 teaspoon kosher salt
¼ teaspoon white pepper
6 tablespoons olive oil
12 pocketless pitas

Preheat the oven to 350°F.

Combine the edamame, tahini, garlic, lemon juice, salt, pepper, and 1 tablespoon water in a food processor. Pulse the ingredients while slowly pouring the olive oil in through the feed tube. Process until the mixture is smooth. Set aside.

Using varying sizes of shamrock-shaped cookie cutters, cut shamrock shapes out of the pitas and place them on a baking sheet. Toast in the oven until golden, about 5 minutes. Serve warm with the hummus.

These are a big hit with little and big folks alike—who doesn't love a "crust" made with ham? It bakes up into a beautiful, organic cup for tender eggs studded with spinach and mozzarella. Serve these with green fruit on a stick.

Makes 6

green eggs & ham PINCH POTS

4 ounces Black Forest ham, thinly sliced

6 large eggs

1 cup spinach, finely chopped

¼ cup shredded mozzarella cheese

⅜ teaspoon kosher salt

¼ teaspoon black pepper

Preheat the oven to 375°F. Coat six wells of a muffin tin with cooking spray. Line each well with slices of ham to cover entirely. In a large bowl, combine the eggs with 1 tablespoon water and whisk until frothy. Stir in the spinach and cheese. Season with the salt and pepper. Spoon the egg mixture into the cups and bake until the eggs have set and the ham is crispy, about 20 minutes. Let cool slightly, then serve warm with fruit skewers.

We don't usually recommend eating monochromatic food (read: white food) but in the case of green, it's a different story.

Makes 8 skewers

green fruit ON A STICK

1 cup green grapes

2 green apples, cored and cut into wedges

2 kiwis, peeled and cut into 8 pieces each

Assemble skewers by alternating grapes, apple wedges, and pieces of kiwi.

Fruit Gazpacho with
Basil & Mint

Grilled Veggie Rainbows
on a Stick

Honey Granola Breakfast Parfait

Tropical Green Smoothie

APRIL

Mini Broccoli Cheddar
Bread Puddings

Lemon-Poppy Seed Cupcakes

Mini Bagel Buffet with
Two Cream Cheeses

Egg Flowers

When April arrives, all my attention turns to the farmers' markets. Going to them at this time of year in California is an exercise in optimism and hope: colorful vegetables begin a gradual return, and big, fat, juicy strawberries make their first appearance. I always take the kids to the market with me—it opens up a dialogue about where our food comes from, who grows it, and how it's grown.

There's nothing like watching a child engage with a farmer: you can see the wheels turning in his or her head, making the connection between that delicious stalk of asparagus and the place where it was planted, nurtured, and plucked from the earth. This is so important; it gets kids excited about trying new fruits and vegetables without your having to cajole and coerce them. Farm it out, I say! At home, we grow lots of tomatoes, most herbs, and, of course, kale. It's a modest assortment, but it's manageable for us, which is key. If all you can handle is a pot of herbs on a windowsill, so be it. Each time you pick some, you'll be reminded of the miracle of dirt, water, sun, and seed.

Earth DAY

In LA, we encounter the consequences of global
warming on a daily basis. The water situation is
precarious, which, of course, touches all our lives.
Frankly, Earth Day is every day around our house!
We started the conversation with our kids early on—
reminding them to conserve, reuse, and recycle as
we cook and go through our day-to-day lives.

Sweet, savory, hot (if you prefer), cool, spicy, crunchy—there's something for everyone in this bright, colorful soup. We are lucky to live in California, where these fresh fruits and vegetables (we grow cucumbers in our backyard) are available in April. Choose produce that is ripe and seasonal where you live. Be sure to taste the gazpacho before serving; chilled dishes often need additional seasoning—a pinch of salt and a splash of vinegar—to brighten the flavors.

Serves 6

Fruit gazpacho
WITH BASIL & MINT

- 2 cups fresh orange juice
- 1½ cups finely diced seedless watermelon
- 1 cup finely diced strawberries
- 1 cup finely diced peaches
- 1 medium tomato, halved, seeded, and diced
- 1 Persian cucumber, or ½ English cucumber, finely diced
- 1 jalapeño, seeded and minced (optional)
- ¼ cup finely chopped sweet onion
- 2 tablespoons extra-virgin olive oil, plus more for garnish
- 1½ tablespoons chopped fresh basil
- 1½ tablespoons chopped fresh mint, plus more for garnish
- 1 tablespoon red wine vinegar
- ½ teaspoon kosher salt

Combine all the ingredients in a large glass pitcher and chill for at least 2 hours and up to 24. Taste and adjust the seasonings. Ladle the gazpacho into clear drinking glasses and drizzle a little olive oil over each. Garnish with mint and serve chilled.

Gia's son started life off as a great eater, but by the time he turned five, things were headed in the other direction. It didn't take long for Gia to figure out that if she put vegetables on a stick (because, let's face it, a stick is compelling to the under-ten set), he would gobble them up. Create a healthy rainbow by arranging brightly colored vegetables on skewers, from red to violet. Choose a combination of any or all of the following.

Makes 8 skewers

GRILLED Veggie Rainbows on a STICK

FOR THE MARINADE

¾ cup olive oil

¼ cup red wine vinegar

1 tablespoon Dijon mustard

1 teaspoon fresh thyme

1 teaspoon chopped fresh rosemary

½ teaspoon garlic salt

½ teaspoon black pepper

FOR THE VEGETABLES

4 pounds assorted vegetables, cut into 2-inch pieces: cherry tomatoes; carrots; sweet potatoes; red, green, orange, and yellow bell peppers; zucchini; summer squash; eggplant; red onion; purple potatoes

Soak 8 wooden skewers in water for at least 30 minutes.

TO MAKE THE MARINADE: Whisk together all of the marinade ingredients in a small bowl and set aside.

TO MAKE THE VEGETABLES: If you're using potatoes, parboil them in salted water for about 10 minutes.

Drain the skewers. Divide the vegetable pieces among the skewers, threading each with a variety of colors. Brush the vegetables with a generous amount of the marinade and let sit for at least 15 minutes.

Meanwhile, heat a charcoal or gas grill to high, or heat a grill pan over high heat until hot. Grill the skewers until the vegetables are softened and have grill marks, 3 to 5 minutes on each side. Serve warm.

HONEY GRANOLA
breakfast parfait

The ingredients in granola range far and wide—this one is oat, almond, and honey based, with some dried fruit tossed in. Granola, for the most part, is like quiche: you can throw in whatever ingredients you have on hand. We love sunflower seeds, pumpkin seeds, shaved coconut, puffed rice, almost any nut, fresh mint, and a fresh berry topping.

Makes 6 parfaits

3 cups old-fashioned rolled oats

1 cup chopped almonds

⅔ cups flaxseeds

⅓ cup coconut oil

½ cup honey, plus more for drizzling

¼ cup packed brown sugar

1½ teaspoons pure vanilla extract

½ teaspoon kosher salt

¾ cup dried cranberries or apricots

3 cups plain Greek yogurt

Fresh fruit, such as apples, pears, and berries, cut into ½-inch pieces

Preheat the oven to 375°F. Line a baking sheet with parchment paper.

Combine the oats, almonds, and flaxseeds in a large bowl and set aside. In a small saucepan, combine the oil, honey, brown sugar, vanilla, and salt, and cook over low heat until the sugar has melted, about 5 minutes. Pour the honey mixture over the oat mixture and stir until thoroughly coated. Spread the mixture in a thin layer on the prepared baking sheet and bake for 20 to 25 minutes, tossing two or three times. Let cool completely. Add the dried fruit, tossing to incorporate.

To make the parfaits, layer the granola, yogurt, and fresh fruit in six mason jars or other glass containers, repeating the layers twice in each one. Drizzle honey over each and serve. Store any leftover granola in an airtight container at room temperature.

Juice bars seem to be as common as banks and pharmacies in LA these days. Gia is currently obsessed with a mixture of almond butter, granola, dates, almond milk, and a splash of vanilla. For Earth Day, celebrate what Mother Nature has wrought with an appropriately green drink that not only tastes delicious but is also loaded with nutrients. It's a great way to start the day and makes an excellent pick-me-up in the late afternoon or for an after-school snack. Use baby spinach whenever possible—it's softer and more tender than the larger leaves.

Makes one 16-ounce or two 8-ounce moothies

TROPICAL green smoothie

- 1 cup baby spinach
- 1 banana
- ¾ cup frozen mango
- ¾ cup frozen pineapple
- ¾ cup coconut water, plus more if needed
- ½ cup kale, chopped

Combine all the ingredients in a blender and blend on high until smooth, about 1 minute. If the smoothie is too thick, gradually add more coconut water, about 1 tablespoon at a time. Pour into a mason jar or glass and serve immediately.

Ringing in SPRING

Brunch seems to be synonymous with spring;
the day has gotten going just enough to warm the patio
and eating outside is back to being a novelty after
the winter hibernation. The dishes here can all be made
ahead: spread them out on a buffet table, serve some
good coffee, and enjoy the morning.

MINI BROCCOLI CHEDDAR *bread puddings*

Pint-size *anything* has a certain kind of charm, especially when it comes to dishes as rich and delicious as bread pudding. These make ideal al fresco brunch food as part of a buffet—adults can eat them off a plate with other offerings, and kids can hold them in one hand while running around. No fork, spoon, or plate required!

Makes 12 puddings

1 tablespoon olive oil
2 garlic cloves, minced
2 cups chopped broccoli
3 scallions, finely chopped
½ teaspoon kosher salt
¼ teaspoon black pepper
1½ cups milk
5 cups cubed (1-inch) brioche
1 large egg
1½ cups shredded cheddar cheese

Preheat the oven to 350°F. Line a 12-cup muffin tin with cupcake liners and coat the liners with cooking spray.

Heat the olive oil in a large skillet over medium-high heat. Add the garlic and sauté until fragrant, about 2 minutes. Add the broccoli and scallions, season with the salt and pepper, and sauté until the scallions are translucent, about 5 minutes. Add the milk and reduce the heat to bring the mixture to a simmer. Simmer for 10 minutes. Remove from the heat and let cool slightly.

Meanwhile, place the bread cubes in a large bowl. Pour the milk mixture over and toss. Whisk the egg in a small bowl and add it to the bread mixture, gently tossing to thoroughly mix. Add the cheese and toss again. Divide the mixture among the prepared muffin cups and bake until golden, about 25 minutes. Serve warm.

There's nothing more welcome after the winter months than a burst of sunshine, which is what these classic treats both look and taste like. Edible flowers are available at most gourmet supermarkets or online; be sure that you use only those that have not been sprayed. Note that we use a purchased cake mix; you'll need additional ingredients to make it.

Makes 24 cupcakes

Lemon- POPPY SEED Cupcakes

1 (15-ounce) box vanilla cake mix

1 (3.4-ounce) box lemon pudding mix

2 tablespoons lemon zest, plus more for garnish

3 tablespoons poppy seeds

Vanilla Buttercream (page 26)

Edible flowers, for garnish (optional)

Preheat the oven to the temperature indicated on the cake mix package. Line two 12-cup muffin tins with paper liners.

In a large bowl, combine the cake mix and the pudding mix. Make the batter according to the directions on the cake mix package, then add the lemon zest and poppy seeds and stir until just blended. Divide the mixture between the prepared muffin tins and bake for 15 to 17 minutes, or until a toothpick inserted into a cupcake comes out clean. Transfer to a wire rack to cool completely before frosting.

Once cooled, frost with the buttercream and garnish with lemon zest or edible flowers.

MINI bagel buffet WITH Two CREAM CHEESES

This assemble-and-serve brunch is ideal for last-minute gatherings. There's so little preparation involved, yet it will look like you've spent all morning pulling it together. Arrange an assortment of mini bagels on a platter with accompanying dishes of sliced tomato, red onion, avocado slices, smoked salmon, and the flavored cream cheeses on page 91. Make a few bagel sandwiches and skewer them to guide your guests.

Whipped Strawberry Cream Cheese

1 (8-ounce) package cream cheese, at room temperature

⅓ cup chopped strawberries

1 tablespoon plus 1 teaspoon strawberry preserves

Combine all the ingredients in a bowl and beat with an electric mixer until light and fluffy. Transfer to a serving bowl. The cream cheese can be made in advance, tightly covered, and stored in the refrigerator for up to 1 week.

Makes a hefty cup

Lemony Herbed Cream Cheese

1 (8-ounce) package cream cheese, at room temperature

1 tablespoon chopped fresh chives

1 tablespoon fresh dill fronds

2 teaspoons lemon zest

Combine all the ingredients in a bowl and mix together with a rubber spatula until thoroughly incorporated. Transfer to a serving bowl. The cream cheese can be made in advance, tightly covered, and stored in the refrigerator for up to 1 week.

Makes a hefty cup

EGG
flowers

Egg molds are ideal for showing off your creativity in the kitchen. Just crack an egg into one (they are available in many shapes) and you have a special breakfast—Just. Like. That.

Makes 1 flower

1 large egg

Spray a skillet and a flower-shaped egg mold with cooking spray. Place the skillet over medium heat and set the mold in the center. Once the pan is hot, crack the egg into the mold and cook until the egg white is opaque and firm, 1 to 2 minutes. Remove the mold and serve if sunny-side up is desired. Alternatively, carefully flip the egg over and cook for 30 seconds to 1 minute more.

Tie Fighter Cheese Snacks

Light Saber Snack Mix

Chewie Cookies

Cheesy Rice & Bean Cakes

Crudités with a Trio of Dips

MAY

Cactus Quesadillas

Smoky Chicken Tortilla Soup

Egg Scramble with
Ruffled Bacon

A Bouquet of Vegetable Flowers & Dip

Bite-size Pancake Muffins

May is a month of

M holidays, with Cinco de Mayo, a commemoration of the Mexican Army's victory over the French in the mid-1800s that has morphed into a celebration of Mexican American culture on May 5 and, of course, Mother's Day. Both are our kind of holidays because, yes, food is the main event. May seems like an appropriate time to indulge my love of *Star Wars*, too. This makes sense as the first movie was released just a month after I was born. Perhaps it is a testament to the story that *Star Wars* was still going strong when I became an actress, and actually played the role of Sith Lord to Freddie's Jedi in *Star Wars Rebel*.

Gia and I had a great time coming up with clever ways to present our favorite Mexican food. A cookie cutter turns a traditional quesadilla into the shape of a cactus; a muffin tin stands in as a handy serving platter for multiple dips and is also the vessel in which we bake cheesy bean cakes that require only your hands to eat. Our *Star Wars*–themed menu is entirely focused on snacks: cheese and crackers, cookies, and snack mix. Preparing it requires little more than a cookie cutter to create the likeness of Chewbacca. When it came to planning Mother's Day, our inspiration began with a bouquet of edible flowers, the petals cut from colorful Holland peppers and the centers black olives and cherry tomatoes. We both agree that this was among our—and we hope your—favorite food crafting moments.

star wars day

It's the ultimate tale of good versus evil, which is why kids, adults, and everyone in between love *Star Wars*. At my house, it's especially beloved, of course. What other kids can say their mom and dad were voices in a *Star Wars* series? We've devised a few theme-appropriate snacks for a *Star Wars* marathon that, of course, can happen any month of the year!

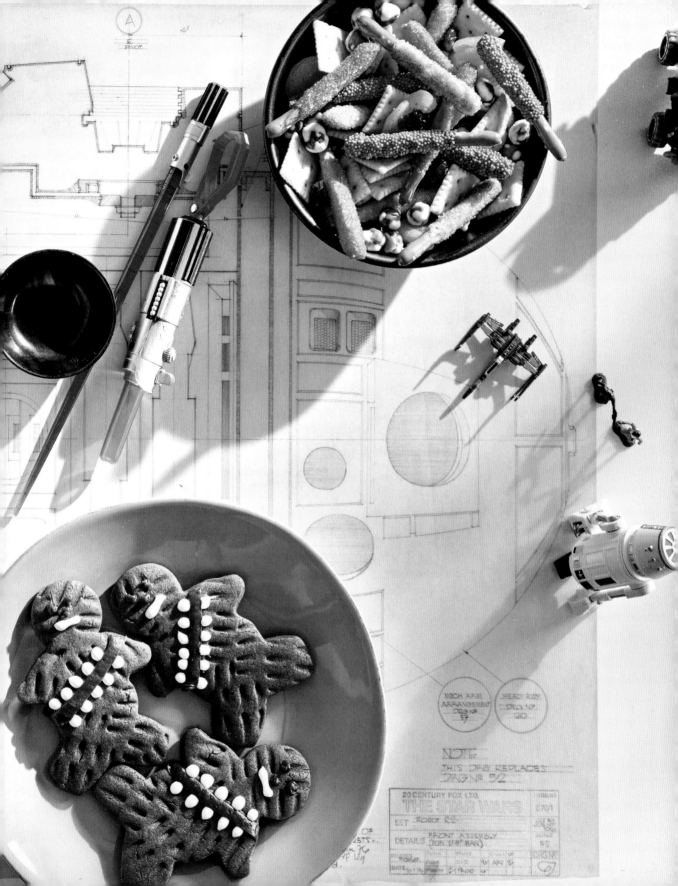

Makes 24 snacks

TIE FIGHTER cheese snacks

¼ cup cream cheese, at room temperature

48 hexagon-shaped crackers

24 (½-inch) cubes colby cheese

Cover the center of one side of each cracker with a thin layer of cream cheese. Press a cube of cheese on top of the cream cheese. Press another cracker on top of the cheese, pressing lightly to adhere. Serve them standing up so they look like TIE fighters. Serve immediately.

Salty, sweet, crunchy, chewy, and just a little bit creamy (thanks to the white chocolate), this is our *Star Wars* version of Chex snack mix. Seek out naturally dyed sprinkles if possible.

Serves 8

Light saber Snack mix

- 2 cups white chocolate chips
- 2 cups pretzel sticks
  - Red, green, or blue sprinkles
- 2 cups mini saltine crackers
- 1 cup wasabi peas
- 1 cup chopped dried fruit

Line a baking sheet with parchment paper. Microwave the chocolate chips in a 2-cup glass measuring cup for 1 to 2 minutes, stirring at 20-second intervals, until melted and smooth. One at a time, partially dip the pretzels into the chocolate, allowing excess chocolate to drip off. Immediately roll the pretzels in sprinkles and place them on the prepared baking sheet. Let stand for 3 to 4 hours, or until firm.

Combine the dipped pretzels, crackers, peas, and fruit in a large bowl and serve.

Chewie COOKIES

We use the tines of a fork to "rough up" the raw dough, which gives these big guys Chewbacca's signature fur coat.

Makes 30 cookies

5½ cups all-purpose flour

1 tablespoon ground ginger

2 teaspoons ground cinnamon

1½ teaspoons baking soda

¼ teaspoon kosher salt

¼ teaspoon ground cloves

⅛ teaspoon ground nutmeg

¼ cup hot water

1 cup molasses

1 cup (2 sticks) unsalted butter, at room temperature

1 cup sugar

½ cup chocolate chips, melted

½ cup white chocolate chips, melted

In a large bowl, whisk together the flour, ginger, cinnamon, baking soda, salt, cloves, and nutmeg. In a medium bowl, stir together the hot water and molasses.

In the bowl of a stand mixer fitted with the paddle attachment, beat the butter and sugar on medium speed until fluffy.

With the mixer running on low speed, gradually add the flour mixture to the butter mixture alternately with the molasses mixture, beginning and ending with the flour mixture. Turn the dough out onto a work surface and shape it into a 1-inch-thick disk. Wrap with waxed paper and chill in the refrigerator for at least 1 hour or up to 2 days.

Preheat the oven to 350°F. Line two baking sheets with parchment paper.

On a lightly floured surface, roll the chilled dough to ¼-inch thickness. Cut the dough with a 3- or 4-inch gingerbread man-shaped cookie cutter. Press the dough with the tines of a fork to create a furry texture. Place the cookies 2 inches apart on the prepared baking sheets.

Bake for 15 to 18 minutes. Let cool on the baking sheets for 5 minutes, then transfer to wire racks to cool completely. Decorate the cookies with the melted chocolate.

cinco de mayo

Freddie and I were married in a small town in Mexico, which is only part (but a big part) of the reason I love the country so much. The other part has something to do with a certain delicious drink that hails from the place (think: salted rim). At another time in my life, I spent several months on a movie set there and was able to live more like a resident than a visitor by browsing in museums, eating with locals, and taking in theater performances. These days, neither of us need an excuse to eat Mexican food or sip a margarita; in California, the Mexican cuisine is the best to be found outside of Mexico. These recipes are meant to get the whole family into the spirit of this festive holiday.

This is what we affectionately call a dump-and-stir recipe, which ultimately means it's truly as easy as that to put together! But even more appealing is that you can eat it straight out of your hand.

Makes 12 cakes

CHEESY rice & bean CAKES

1 (13.8-ounce) package refrigerated pizza dough

2 cups grated sharp cheddar cheese

1 (15-ounce) can black beans, drained and rinsed

1 cup cooked white rice

1 cup jarred salsa

¼ cup chopped fresh cilantro, plus more for garnish

2 scallions, thinly sliced

Sour cream, for serving

Preheat the oven to 375°F. Line a 12-cup muffin tin with decorative paper liners.

Remove the dough from the package. On a lightly floured surface, roll out the dough into a 9×12-inch rectangle and cut it into twelve 3-inch squares. Stretch the squares gently and place one in each prepared muffin cup, pressing them slightly up and over the sides. Set aside.

In a medium bowl, combine 1¼ cups of the cheese, the beans, rice, salsa, cilantro, and scallions. Divide the mixture evenly among the muffin cups. Sprinkle the remaining ¾ cup cheese over the tops of the cakes. Bake until golden brown, about 20 minutes. Set aside to cool slightly before serving.

crudités

~ WITH A ~
TRIO OF dips

We raided the baking drawer when it came to finding serving pieces for this classic hors d'oeuvre; divide the three dips among a 12-cup muffin tin and arrange the vegetables on a baking sheet. So easy to carry from the kitchen to the backyard! Choose whatever vegetables are freshest; here we sliced young carrots and Persian cucumbers lengthwise and peeled leaves away from a head of radicchio.

Guacamole

3 large ripe avocados, pitted and peeled

1 tablespoon fresh lemon juice

1 tablespoon fresh lime juice

½ cup seeded and diced tomato

½ cup finely chopped red onion

1 jalapeño, seeded and finely chopped

Kosher salt

In a medium bowl, mash the avocados with a fork. Add the lemon and lime juice and stir thoroughly. In a separate medium bowl, combine the tomato, onion, and jalapeño and mix until thoroughly incorporated. Season with salt as needed. Spoon the guacamole into four of the muffin cups. Divide the tomato mixture among them.

Mango Tomato Salsa

1 cup cubed mango

1 cup seeded and chopped tomato

½ cup chopped red onion

½ cup peeled and chopped cucumber

¼ cup fresh cilantro, coarsely chopped

1 jalapeño, seeded and chopped (optional)

2 to 3 tablespoons fresh lime juice

Kosher salt and black pepper

Lime wedges, for garnish

Combine the mango, tomato, onion, cucumber, cilantro, jalapeño, and lime juice in a bowl and toss thoroughly. Season with salt and pepper. Spoon the mixture into four muffin cups and garnish each with a lime wedge.

Cilantro-Lime Crema

1 cup sour cream

½ cup finely chopped fresh cilantro, plus leaves for garnish

2 tablespoons fresh lime juice

Combine all the ingredients in a medium bowl and stir until thoroughly combined. Cover and refrigerate until chilled through. Spoon the mixture into four muffin cups and garnish with cilantro leaves.

A cool way
to serve
CLASSIC
crudité.

We love the idea of a cactus-shaped quesadilla, but any other holiday-appropriate shape will do. A sombrero, the number 5, or a guitar, would all work well. Use metal cookie cutters if possible; they have sharp edges that will easily cut through the tortillas.

This recipe is for the classic cheese version, but fillings like chopped chile peppers, caramelized onions, chopped baby spinach, chorizo, and shredded roasted chicken make great additions.

Makes about 12 quesadillas

CACTUS Quesadillas

1 cup shredded sharp cheddar cheese

1 cup shredded Monterey Jack cheese

1 cup shredded colby cheese

3 tablespoons unsalted butter, at room temperature

6 large flour tortillas

In a medium bowl, combine the cheeses and toss to combine. Butter one side of each tortilla. Place the tortilla, buttered-side down, in a large skillet over medium-high heat. Place ½ cup of the cheese mix on the tortilla. Once the cheese begins to melt, fold the tortilla in half and, using a spatula, flip it over. Cook until both sides are golden brown. Transfer to a platter and cover with a kitchen towel to keep warm. Repeat with the remaining cheese and tortillas. Using a cactus cookie cutter (or another cookie cutter of your choice), cut two cacti from each quesadilla. Serve warm.

SMOKY Chicken TORTILLA SOUP

Part of the fun of eating this lively soup is experimenting with some or all of the toppings that are traditionally served with it: chopped cilantro, shredded cheddar cheese, sliced jalapeños, chunks of avocados, and lime wedges for squeezing. There are the tortilla strips, too, of course, which provide an essential crunch. For a heartier meal, serve the soup with wedges of cornbread. The soup can be frozen, tightly covered, for up to 1 month.

Serves 8 to 10

1 tablespoon vegetable oil

2 pounds boneless, skinless chicken thighs

1 large onion, chopped

1 celery stalk, thinly sliced

3 garlic cloves, finely chopped

2 teaspoons chili powder

2 teaspoons smoked paprika

2 teaspoons ground cumin

2 teaspoons dried oregano

4 cups low-sodium chicken broth

1 (28-ounce) can diced tomatoes

2 (4-ounce) cans diced green chiles

½ cup chopped fresh cilantro

Juice of 1 lime

Kosher salt and black pepper

4 (5½-inch) corn tortillas

Heat the oil in a large Dutch oven over medium-high heat. Working in batches, cook the chicken until the juices run clear when the meat is pierced with a fork, about 5 minutes on each side. Using a slotted spoon, transfer the chicken to a plate to cool. Once the chicken is cool enough to handle, shred it with your hands and set aside.

In the same pot, sauté the onion and celery until tender and fragrant, about 5 minutes. Add the garlic, chili powder, paprika, cumin, and oregano and sauté until fragrant, about 1 minute. Stir in the broth, and the tomatoes and green chiles with their juices, scraping up any browned bits on the bottom of the pot. Stir in the shredded chicken. Cover and bring to a boil; then reduce heat to medium and simmer for 45 minutes. Stir in the cilantro and lime juice and season with salt and pepper.

Meanwhile, preheat the oven to 375°F. Cut the tortillas into ¼-inch-wide strips and place them on a baking sheet. Bake for 5 minutes. Toss and continue baking until crisp, about 5 minutes more. Season with salt.

Ladle the soup into mason jars (or bowls, of course!) and serve with the tortilla strips and toppings of your choice.

Mother's day

We both believe that mothers should be celebrated
365 days a year, but we are daughters as well as mothers, so
we love feting our own moms on this one special day. Gia's
mother (and grandmother!) visit her faithfully
on this holiday and center the celebration around an
exquisite yet simple breakfast. Some of the most
treasured gifts we've received are handmade or homemade
by our kids. I am treated to tiny chocolate chip pancakes
and Gia's son has become an expert coffee maker
and loves to present her with a beautiful, piping-hot mug
with frothy milk on top.

There is bacon and eggs, and then there is this version that's perfect for beloved mothers. By simply threading a piece of bacon onto a wooden skewer, you show that you've taken time out to create a special treat for her. And most mothers we know would much rather eat breakfast out of a jar than on a fancy piece of china. Serve this on a tray with a small bunch of her favorite flowers.

Serves 4

Egg scramble
with RUFFLED BACON

8 thick-cut bacon slices

8 large eggs

2 tablespoons milk or water

Kosher salt and black pepper

1 cup shredded cheddar cheese

1 avocado, pitted, peeled, and sliced

Soak eight 8-inch wooden skewers in water for 30 minutes. Drain.

Preheat the oven to 400°F. Line a baking sheet with aluminum foil and place a wire rack on top.

Thread each piece of bacon onto its own wooden skewer and place them on the rack, spacing them ½ inch apart. Bake until the bacon is crispy, about 30 minutes.

Meanwhile, in a large bowl, whisk together the eggs and milk. Coat a skillet with cooking spray and set it over medium heat. Pour the eggs into the pan and season with salt and pepper. After 30 seconds, begin scraping the bottom of the pan with a rubber spatula. Cook, scraping often, and stir in the cheese before the eggs are fully set. Fill mason jars with the scrambled eggs and top with avocado. Stick two bacon skewers into each jar.

A BOUQUET OF Vegetable flowers AND DIP

Our kids love making these—they're simple to make, but the payoff is big (and delicious). The herbed buttermilk dip can be made in advance, covered tightly, and stored in the refrigerator for up to 3 days.

Makes 4 flowers and 1 cup dip

FOR THE FLOWERS

2 large red bell peppers, halved, ribs and seeds removed

2 large yellow bell peppers, halved, ribs and seeds removed

4 (½-inch-thick) slices peeled cucumber

4 grape tomatoes

4 black olives, pitted

FOR THE DIP

1 cup plain Greek yogurt

2 tablespoons buttermilk

2 tablespoons chopped fresh parsley

2 teaspoons onion powder

1½ teaspoons finely chopped fresh chives

1½ teaspoons garlic powder

1¼ teaspoons fresh dill fronds

1 teaspoon kosher salt

¾ teaspoon black pepper

TO MAKE THE FLOWERS: Set the pepper halves on a work surface skin-side down. Using two flower-shaped cookie cutters in graduated sizes and that will fit onto the halved peppers, cut out flowers, alternating the sizes and colors. Using an appropriately sized flower cutter, cut out flowers from the cucumber rounds. Thread the vegetables onto skewers, beginning with a grape tomato, followed by a cucumber, a smaller pepper flower, and finally a larger pepper flower. Top the skewer with an olive. Arrange the flowers in a glass jar and set aside.

TO MAKE THE DIP: Combine all the ingredients in a medium bowl and whisk until thoroughly incorporated. Cover and refrigerate until ready to serve.

Place the bouquet of flowers and the dip on a tray and serve.

We can say with certainty that this is a recipe kids love to make and moms love to eat. Gia's son regularly bakes these up, doctoring them with bananas or fresh berries. But chocolate chips are a mainstay. Keep in mind that you will need additional ingredients (eggs, etc.) to make the packaged pancakes.

Makes about forty-eight 2-inch pancakes

BITE-SIZE
Pancake Muffins

1 (20-ounce) box pancake mix

½ cup blueberries

1 banana, thinly sliced crosswise

½ cup chocolate chips

Pure maple syrup

Preheat the oven to 375°F. Spray two mini-muffin tins with cooking spray.

Prepare the pancake mix according to the package directions. Spoon a tablespoon of batter into each cup of the prepared muffin tins. Divide the bananas and blueberries among them. Top with a few chocolate chips.

Bake until the muffins have puffed up and a toothpick inserted into the center comes out clean, about 15 minutes. Put the maple syrup in small bowls and serve.

Tomatoes by the Spoonful

Chicken Pasta Salad

Coconut Chicken Fingers

Pineapple - Lime
"Snow Cones"

JUNE

Nest Eggs

Alphabet Fruit

Grilled Cheese Silk Ties

#1 Dad Loaf Cake

This month

contains the longest day of the year, which makes it official: summer has begun in earnest. It's time to loosen up, relax, kick off your shoes, and get a little sand between your toes. Eating outdoors is the rule rather than the exception, and every meal feels like a celebration of the season's bounty. Gia has long celebrated the start of summer with a solstice gathering that friends and family have come to mark on their calendars months in advance. It's a completely low-key affair, one that leaves her free to enjoy the party. An easy fresh tomato salad, a vibrant pasta salad, and chicken fingers coated with coconut for the kids are on the menu, with refreshing shaved ice for dessert. It's a meal to replicate throughout the warm months—a go-to in keeping with the casual vibe of the season.

In our Father's Day menu, we created one of our clever edible "bowls" from shredded potatoes pressed into muffin tins to form a nest in which a tasty bite of sausage and an egg perch. Between that, the grilled cheese sandwiches shaped like ties, and fruit letters arranged to spell out a sentimental message, we're pretty sure Dad will be charmed beyond measure.

summer
solstice

When Gia was a teenager, she moved from Nevada to New York City, where she instantly absorbed the feeling that washes over all New Yorkers as soon as the weather turns nice. City folk just can't get enough of the glorious weather. Summer is cherished unlike any other season—the city is less crowded, the days are longer, eating al fresco is the norm, and everyone seems to be breathing just a little easier.

There's no better way to celebrate the season than with summer tomatoes and basil from the garden, except to eat them straight from a glass with a spoon. Use the best, freshest ingredients you can find, since there are so few here and they are served fresh.

Serves 4

tomatoes BY THE spoonful

1 pint baby yellow pear tomatoes, halved

1 pint Sun Gold tomatoes, halved

1 (16-ounce) container bocconcini mozzarella cheese, drained and halved

½ cup fresh basil leaves, coarsely chopped

3 tablespoons white balsamic vinegar

2 teaspoons Dijon mustard

1 teaspoon kosher salt

¼ teaspoon black pepper

⅓ cup extra-virgin olive oil

Combine the tomatoes, bocconcini, and basil in a medium bowl and toss. In a small bowl, combine the vinegar, mustard, salt, and pepper. While whisking, slowly stream in the olive oil and whisk until emulsified. Pour the dressing over the tomato mixture until everything is coated. Spoon the mixture into four glasses and serve.

A room-temperature salad is always a crowd-pleaser on a summer table; Broccolini and zucchini keep it bright and colorful.

Makes about 8 servings

CHICKEN pasta salad

1 pound fusilli

¾ cup plus 1 tablespoon extra-virgin olive oil

1 teaspoon minced garlic

2 cups coarsely chopped Broccolini

4 small zucchini, quartered lengthwise and cut crosswise into 2-inch pieces

Kosher salt and black pepper

¼ cup red wine vinegar

1 tablespoon fresh lemon juice

2 teaspoons Dijon mustard

2 large rotisserie chicken breasts, skin removed, diced

⅓ cup pine nuts, toasted

4 ounces crumbled feta cheese

Bring a large pot of salted water to a boil and cook the pasta according to the package directions. Drain.

Meanwhile, heat 1 tablespoon of the olive oil over medium heat. Add ½ teaspoon of the minced garlic. Add the Broccolini and cook until it brightens, 2 to 3 minutes. Add the zucchini and sauté until it softens, about 5 minutes. Season with salt and pepper and remove from the heat.

Combine the vinegar, lemon juice, mustard, and remaining ½ teaspoon garlic in a small bowl. While whisking, slowly stream in the remaining ¾ cup olive oil and whisk until emulsified. Season with salt and pepper.

Combine the pasta, vegetables, and chicken in a large bowl and toss. Pour the dressing over and mix until well coated. Add the pine nuts and feta and toss once again. Transfer the pasta salad to a large glass jar or vase and serve at room temperature.

Gia created these for her son and his friends,
but it seems the adults can't get enough of them.
Make twice as many as you think you'll need!

Serves 6

COCONUT chicken fingers

3 egg whites

½ cup cornstarch

1 teaspoon garlic salt

1 teaspoon black pepper

1 cup sweetened flaked coconut

1 cup panko bread crumbs

½ teaspoon kosher salt

1 teaspoon paprika

12 chicken breast tenders

Red pepper jelly

Preheat the oven to 425°F.

In a small bowl, whisk the egg whites just until foamy. In a shallow dish, stir together the cornstarch, garlic salt, and ½ teaspoon of the pepper. In a separate shallow dish, stir together the coconut, bread crumbs, salt, paprika, and remaining ½ teaspoon pepper.

Working one at a time, dredge the chicken tenders first in the cornstarch mixture, then dip them in the egg whites, and finally dredge them in the coconut mixture, pressing it gently with your fingers to adhere. Skewer the chicken tenders, if desired, then coat them generously on each side with cooking spray; arrange them on a wire rack set over a baking sheet.

Bake until golden and the chicken is opaque when pierced, 12 to 15 minutes, turning once after 8 minutes. Serve warm with red pepper jelly.

Here's a healthier version of the sugary shaved ice synonymous with country fairs and city vendors. You can substitute any other citrus juice for the lime juice.

Serves 4 to 6

PINEAPPLE-LIME "snow cones"

¼ cup fresh lime juice (from 2 limes)

⅓ cup sugar

2 cups pineapple juice

2 teaspoons lime zest

Combine the lime juice, sugar, and ¾ cup water in a 4-cup glass measuring cup. Microwave on High for 2 minutes or until the sugar has dissolved. Let cool completely. Stir in the pineapple juice and lime zest. Pour the syrup into a 9 x 13-inch baking pan. Cover tightly with plastic wrap and freeze for 6 hours or until completely firm. Scrape the frozen mixture with the tines of a fork until flaky. Return the pan to the freezer and freeze for 2 hours more. Scrape again until the ice crystals are light and fluffy. Serve immediately in paper cups.

Father's DAY

Father's Day holds a very special place for me.
My husband lost his father, Freddie Prinze, at a young age, and
in the years before we had children, the day was anything but
festive. Now that Freddie Jr. and I have our own children, the
atmosphere has changed dramatically. The kids and I spoil him to
pieces on his day. My son devotes the whole day to Dad.
He especially loves serving the Grilled Cheese Silk Ties!

These are a wonderful way to make eggs for a crowd. They are "tastefully" contained in a shredded potato nest that turns crispy when baked.

Makes 12 nests

Nest Eggs

6 ounces bulk sweet Italian sausage, casings removed

5 cups shredded peeled potatoes, set into a colander

4 egg whites

1 tablespoon olive oil

1 teaspoon kosher salt

½ teaspoon black pepper, plus more as needed

1 cup shredded sharp cheddar cheese

12 large eggs

Preheat the oven to 450°F. Spray a 12-cup muffin tin with cooking spray.

Heat a small skillet over medium heat. Add the sausage and cook, breaking up the meat with a wooden spoon as it cooks, until nicely browned. Set aside.

Use the back of a spoon to press down on the shredded potatoes to remove excess moisture. In a large bowl, combine the potatoes, egg whites, olive oil, salt, and pepper. Place ½ cup of the potato mixture into each prepared muffin cup, firmly pressing against the sides and bottom. Bake for 15 minutes, or until the potatoes are golden. Remove from the oven and place a spoonful each of sausage and cheese in the bottom of each cup. Working one at a time, crack each egg into a small bowl, then transfer it to a muffin cup over the sausage and cheese. Return the tin to the oven. Bake for 8 minutes for over-easy eggs, 10 minutes for over-medium, and 12 minutes for over-hard. Let cool slightly and remove from the muffin tin. Season with some pepper and serve warm.

Spelling it out can be the most poignant way to tell Dad how you feel. And even more so when the letters are cut from luscious melons! Tiny letter cookie cutters or small clay molds are available at arts and crafts supply stores, cookware shops, or online.

Alphabet
FRUIT

Watermelon
Cantaloupe
Honeydew
Blueberries

Cut the melons into 1-inch-thick slices. Using the alphabet cutters, cut out letters to spell desired words or phrases. Slide the letters onto wooden skewers, separating words with a blueberry. Arrange them on the plate as a garnish and serve.

There are grilled cheese sandwiches, and there are Father's Day grilled cheese sandwiches. These not only feature three kinds of cheese, including one with truffles (we use Cypress Grove Chevre from California), but they are cut into the shape of Dad's tie. Arranged on a plate with a sentiment spelled out in fruit, they're certain to charm Dad.

Makes 8

GRILLED CHEESE
silk ties

3 tablespoons unsalted butter

1 teaspoon minced garlic

8 slices whole-grain rustic or artisanal bread

4 teaspoons Dijon mustard

4 ounces Fontina cheese, thinly sliced

4 ounces Asiago cheese, thinly sliced

4 ounces truffled chèvre, crumbled

Alphabet Fruit (page 138), for serving

In a small saucepan, combine the butter and the garlic and melt the butter over medium-low heat. Brush one side of each slice of bread with the melted garlic butter. Spread ½ teaspoon of the mustard on the other side of each slice of bread. Evenly distribute the cheeses onto the mustard side of four slices of bread and top with the other slices, buttered-side up.

In a large skillet, heat the sandwiches over medium heat. Once the cheese begins to melt, use an offset spatula to flip the sandwiches and cook until both sides of the bread are browned and toasted. Using a tie-shaped cookie cutter, cut each sandwich into two ties. Arrange the sandwiches on a plate with Alphabet Fruit alongside.

SPELL *it out*
for Father's
Day.

This was inspired by Foodstirs—we made a baking kit for Father's Day and it was hugely successful, not to mention simple. Our hunch is that it appealed to kids because it is so easy to make. Decorate the cake, of course, but don't ignore the plate. Use the piping bag to "write" a poignant message for Dad. You'll need to use additional ingredients (eggs, etc.) to make the cake.

Makes one 9 x 5-inch loaf

#1 DAD
Loaf Cake

1¼ cups chocolate chips

1 (15.25-ounce) box vanilla cake mix

Vanilla Buttercream (page 26)

Natural food dye in desired color

Preheat the oven according to the cake mix package directions. Spray a 9 x 5-inch loaf pan with cooking spray.

In a small bowl, toss the chocolate chips with 2 tablespoons of the cake mix to prevent them from clumping and falling to the bottom of the pan. Prepare the cake batter as directed, then fold in the coated chocolate chips. Pour the batter into the loaf pan and bake until a toothpick inserted into the center comes out clean, 32 to 35 minutes. Transfer to a wire rack and let cool completely before removing the loaf from the pan.

Divide the buttercream between two bowls. Into one, squeeze a few drops of food coloring and stir until no white streaks remain. Set aside. Using an offset spatula, frost the top of the loaf with the white frosting and place the cake in the freezer for 10 minutes to set the frosting. Spoon the colored frosting into a piping bag fitted with a #7 open-star tip. Pipe decorations onto the cake and, if desired, a message directly onto the serving plate. Bring the cake to room temperature before serving.

Corn Dog "Cupcakes"

Sliders on a Stick

Crunchy Green Bean Fries

S'mores Parfait

JULY

Shark Bite Cupcakes

Shark Bite Sugar Cookies

Shark Fin Parfaits

The month of July

seems to have been created for the kind of eating and entertaining we love. There's levity in the air, the farmers' markets are bursting with gorgeous produce, and the possibilities seem endless. It's the middle of the summer, and we're in the groove.

All over the country on Independence Day, children march in parades, families barbecue, bands play in local parks, and the beaches swell with vacationers. For many, the Fourth is summer's official kickoff, and what better way to do it than with those classic American concoctions, the corn dog and the s'more? Fireworks fly, flags wave, and the food flows, but we are careful to make sure our kids understand the true meaning of the holiday—and that they appreciate the value and beauty of true freedom.

July also brings with it Shark Week, about which I am fanatical. I am obsessed with sharks and always have been. As a result, we had a blast developing slightly off-the-wall creations for the occasion, which we treated like a trial run for Halloween! While supportive of me in every way, Freddie does not share my passion, and my children are still too young to introduce to sharks. So, that *Jaws* marathon will have to wait, but the jiggly parfaits and shark bite cookies are fair game.

Fourth of July

Hang up the flag, break out the sparklers, and pass around the corn dogs and parfaits. Summer is officially here! We celebrate with an open house–style pool party, Freddie fires up the grill, and the menu takes advantage of the height of summer bounty. Gia is often on the East Coast, on Long Island, where an old-fashioned barbecue on the beach is a yearly ritual.

Yes, you can make the carnival staple at home;
all you need is a muffin tin. These are bound to get
gobbled up, so you may want to double the recipe.

Makes 12 "cupcakes"

Corn Dog "Cupcakes"

1 cup all-purpose flour

1 cup yellow cornmeal

1 tablespoon baking powder

1 teaspoon kosher salt

⅓ cup sugar

2 large eggs

1 cup milk

4 tablespoons (½ stick)
 unsalted butter, melted

⅓ cup honey

6 hot dogs, cut into ½-inch
 pieces

Spicy mustard, for serving

Preheat the oven to 400°F. Line a 12-cup muffin tin with paper liners.

Combine the flour, cornmeal, baking powder, salt, and sugar in a large bowl and whisk to blend. In a separate bowl, whisk the eggs. Add the milk, melted butter, and honey to the eggs and continue whisking until well blended. Pour the egg mixture into the flour mixture and whisk until combined.

Divide the batter evenly among the prepared muffin cups. Place a few pieces of hot dog into each cup of batter and bake until a toothpick inserted into the center comes out clean, 15 to 17 minutes. Serve warm with mustard.

In our experience, each guest will eat two of
these—and rather quickly! Plan accordingly.

Makes 12 sliders

Sliders on a stick

1½ pounds ground beef or
  turkey

  Kosher salt and black
  pepper

6 ounces sliced cheddar
  cheese

1½ cups arugula

12 small brioche buns or
  dinner rolls, toasted

2 plum tomatoes, sliced

1 red onion, sliced

12 pickle slices

  Condiments, as desired

Prepare a charcoal or gas grill.

Shape the beef into twelve 2-inch balls and press slightly to flatten
into patties. Liberally season each side with salt and pepper. Place
the sliders on the grill and cook for 3 to 4 minutes, then flip and
cook for 2 to 3 minutes more. Top with the sliced cheese. Cover
the grill and cook for another minute to melt the cheese.

To assemble each slider, place a few arugula leaves on the bottom
bun and top with a burger patty. Place a slice each of tomato,
onion, and pickle on top of the patty and top with the other half
of the bun. Place a skewer through the center of each slider. Serve
warm with the condiments of your choice.

CRUNCHY green bean FRIES

2 cups panko bread crumbs

2 tablespoons canola oil, plus more for greasing

2 teaspoons lemon pepper

¼ cup grated Parmesan cheese

1 large egg

½ cup buttermilk

½ cup all-purpose flour

¾ pound green beans, trimmed

Creamy Dijon mustard, for serving

Preheat the oven to 450°F. Lightly grease two wire racks with canola oil and set each over a baking sheet.

In a shallow bowl, combine the bread crumbs, 2 tablespoons canola oil, and lemon pepper and stir until well coated; stir in the cheese. In another bowl, whisk together the egg and buttermilk. Pour the flour into a third, shallow bowl. Dredge each green bean in the flour, then dip it into the egg mixture, letting any excess drip off, and then coat with bread crumbs, pressing them gently to adhere.

Arrange the breaded green beans in a single layer on the baking racks. Bake until golden brown, about 15 minutes. Arrange the fries in bunches in drinking glasses and serve with mustard for dipping.

Here's a riff on the campfire favorite, made even a bit more decadent with chocolate mousse instead of chocolate bars.

Makes 6 parfaits

S'mores PARFAIT

24 double graham crackers, broken into large pieces

6 cups Chocolate Mousse Pudding (page 47)

30 mini marshmallows

Place a 1-inch layer of graham cracker pieces in the bottom of four 16-ounce jars. Spoon ½ cup of mousse over the graham crackers in each jar. Top with a second layer of graham crackers and another ½ cup of mousse. Top each jar with 5 marshmallows to cover. Using a kitchen torch, toast the marshmallows until golden. Serve immediately.

(If you don't have a kitchen torch, preheat the oven to 400°F and arrange the marshmallows on a parchment paper-lined baking sheet, at least 3 inches apart. Bake for 3 to 5 minutes. Keep an eye on the marshmallows to make sure they don't burn. Use a spatula to remove the marshmallows from the baking sheet and place them in the jars, pressing them slightly into the mousse.)

shark
week

Strawberry preserves make great blood, and azure-blue gelatin could easily be mistaken for the sea. Take a chunk out of a sugar cookie person to mimic a shark bite. We could go on and on. This is the only version of Shark Week my kids have seen so far; they'll have to wait a few years before they can handle the real thing.

Strawberry jam stands in for, well, the inevitable when a shark takes a bite out of these intriguing cupcakes.

Makes 12 cupcakes

shark Bite CUPCAKES

FOR THE CUPCAKES

- 1 (15.25-ounce) box vanilla cake mix
- 1 cup strawberry preserves
- Vanilla Buttercream (page 26)
- Blue sparkling sanding sugar

FOR THE TOPPERS

- Gray construction paper
- Scissors or X-ACTO knife
- Clear glue
- Toothpicks

TO MAKE THE CUPCAKES: Prepare the cupcakes according to the cake mix package directions. Transfer to a wire rack to cool. Spoon the preserves into a piping bag fitted with any tip and use the tip to poke a hole into the top of each cooled cupcake. Fill the centers with the preserves. Using an offset spatula, frost the cupcakes with the buttercream and sprinkle a generous amount of blue sugar on each.

TO MAKE THE TOPPERS: Cut fin shapes out of construction paper. Place a drop of glue in the center of each fin and attach a toothpick. Once glue has dried, place a topper into the center of each cupcake.

These should be reserved for only those
with an excellent sense of humor.

Makes about 20

SHARK BITE *sugar cookies*

- ½ cup (1 stick) butter
- 1 cup sugar
- 1 large egg
- 1¼ teaspoons pure vanilla extract
- ¼ teaspoon kosher salt
- ½ teaspoon baking powder
- 2 cups all-purpose flour, plus more for rolling
- 2 tablespoons strawberry preserves

In the bowl of a stand mixer fitted with the paddle attachment, cream the butter on medium speed. Gradually add the sugar and beat until the mixture is light and fluffy. Add the egg and vanilla and mix until combined, then add the salt and baking powder and mix until incorporated. Slowly pour in the flour and mix until incorporated and a dough forms. Gather the dough into a ball and flatten it into a 1-inch-thick disk. Wrap tightly in plastic wrap and freeze for 30 minutes.

Preheat the oven to 350°F. Line two baking sheets with parchment paper.

Dust a clean work surface with flour and roll out the dough to a ¼-inch thickness. Using shark, surfboard, and gingerbread man cutters, cut out cookies. To create the "shark bites," use an apple corer, X-ACTO knife, or paring knife to cut jagged half circles out of the sides of the surfboards. For the shark bite "victims," cut off an arm or a leg using jagged cuts. Transfer the cookies to the baking sheets and bake until the edges are golden, 8 to 10 minutes. Transfer to a wire rack to cool. Brush a little of the strawberry preserves around the shark bites and in the sharks' mouths.

Blue gelatin makes for a great-looking ocean in these delightful desserts. The shark fins are made out of fondant, which is as fun to shape and mold as Play-Doh. Believe us, you can get carried away with it! Fondant takes a little time to dry—it has to set overnight—so factor that into your game plan.

Serves 8

Shark Fin Parfaits

- 4 cups of white grape juice
- 4 tablespoons gelatin
- 2 tablespoons honey
- 1 to 2 teaspoons of blue dye-free food coloring
- ⅓ cup natural rock candy
- About ¼ cup heavy cream
- 1 teaspoon sugar
- Fondant Shark Fins (recipe follows)

Pour juice into medium saucepan. Add gelatin and stir until dissolved. Place on medium heat and simmer for about 10 minutes. Remove from heat and let cool for 2 minutes. Stir in honey and taste (for a sweeter flavor, add more honey). Add natural blue food dye, a few drops at a time, until desired color is reached.

Divide the rock candy among eight 6- to 8-ounce glass jars. Divide the gelatin among the jars. In a medium bowl, use an electric mixer to beat the cream with the sugar until it holds soft peaks. Top each jar with a dollop of whipped cream and a shark fin.

FONDANT SHARK FINS

Dust a clean work surface with cornstarch. Thinly roll a 2- to 3-inch ball of white fondant into a thin layer. Cut out 8 shark fin shapes, adding fin details if desired. Let dry on a wire rack until hard, at least overnight. Coat with edible glitter and let dry for a few minutes before assembling.

Salad Kebabs

Fresh Corn Pops with
Compound Butters

Fruit Ice Cubes

AUGUST

Strawberry Ice Cream Cupcakes

Sweet Pizza with
Fruit Toppings

Growing up on the East Coast, August meant summer was on, full tilt. Now that I have school-age children and live on the West Coast, I have to pack what was once four weeks of glorious relaxation into two; they start school in mid-August! I try to hold on to that summer feeling for dear life—and get most of it through the delicious food I pull together from summer ingredients.

Caesar salad on a stick? Yes, along with the classic wedge of iceberg with bacon or a refreshing Asian chicken salad—these exemplify the food crafting approach. By deconstructing salads that are traditionally tossed and threading the ingredients onto skewers, we have changed the way it feels to eat a salad. At the height of the summer, when vegetables are in their prime, it's nice to be able to taste a tomato's full flavor, a scallion's sharp bite, and a pure chunk of Parmesan. Summer is for improvisation, and we say go for it.

To that end, our hope is that the sweet pizza in this chapter will inspire you to come up with your own visual tricks. Where pizza dough is expected, we put a sweet cookie with a mix of cream cheese and heavy cream standing in for the mozzarella cheese, and fresh berries are scattered about for the topping. Mini ice cream cakes, made in muffin tins and frosted with whipped cream, are our homemade answer to that childhood favorite, the Carvel ice cream cake. This is the month for soaking it all in—fresh, fun food, sun, sand, salt air, and easy breezes.

summer celebration

To my mind, every day of summer feels like a celebration. Gia appreciates the season intensely, having spent her early childhood in Las Vegas and her adulthood in California, land of the eternal sun. I may have been raised a city girl, but I've never had any trouble adjusting to the beach life of California. We both are acutely aware that September is right around the corner and with that, the start of school and hectic schedules. We devised this menu to take full advantage of the remaining summer days.

Is it really possible to eat salad from a stick? Indeed it is! It's all in the way you chop the ingredients. Serving what is typically a composed dish in a deconstructed way instantly conveys a casual vibe, perfect for the warm months when flatware—and shoes—should be optional at the dinner table.

Makes 8 skewers of each salad

Salad KEBABS

The Classic Wedge with Creamy Gorgonzola Dressing

FOR THE SALAD

- 6 thick-cut bacon slices
- 1 small head iceberg lettuce, cut into 1½-inch pieces
- 9 cherry tomatoes, halved

FOR THE DRESSING

- ½ cup buttermilk
- ⅓ cup mayonnaise
- ¼ cup plain Greek yogurt
- ¼ cup Gorgonzola cheese, crumbled
- Juice of ½ lemon
- 1 teaspoon Worcestershire sauce
- ½ teaspoon garlic powder
- Kosher salt and black pepper

TO MAKE THE SALAD: Preheat the oven to 400°F. Line a baking sheet with aluminum foil and place a wire rack on top. Arrange the bacon on the rack, spacing the slices ½ inch apart. Bake until the bacon is almost crispy, about 20 minutes.

Break each piece of bacon into 4 pieces. To assemble, place a piece of iceberg onto a skewer, followed by a tomato half and a piece of bacon. Repeat this combination twice more and finish with another piece of iceberg. Set on a serving platter. Repeat with the remaining ingredients.

TO MAKE THE DRESSING: In a small bowl, whisk together the buttermilk, mayonnaise, yogurt, cheese, lemon juice, Worcestershire, and garlic powder. Season with the salt and pepper. Drizzle the dressing over the skewers or serve in small bowls for dipping.

Chinese Chicken Salad with Sesame-Ginger Vinaigrette

FOR THE SALAD:

½ head of cabbage, cut into 1½-inch pieces

2 carrots, cut on an angle into ½-inch pieces

2 scallions, cut into 1-inch pieces

2 large rotisserie chicken breasts, skin removed, cut into 1-inch pieces

2 mandarin oranges, peeled and segmented

FOR THE DRESSING

⅓ cup rice vinegar

3 tablespoons honey

3 tablespoons vegetable oil

2 tablespoons sesame oil

1 tablespoon fresh lime juice

2 teaspoons soy sauce

½ teaspoon minced garlic

½ teaspoon minced ginger

Kosher salt and black pepper

TO MAKE THE SALAD: Place a piece of cabbage on a skewer, followed by a slice of carrot, a piece of chicken, and a scallion. Repeat this layering process again and finish with one more piece of cabbage. Set on a platter and repeat with the remaining ingredients.

TO MAKE THE DRESSING: In a small bowl, whisk together the vinegar, honey, vegetable oil, sesame oil, lime juice, soy sauce, garlic, and ginger. Season with salt and pepper.

Drizzle the dressing over the skewers or serve in small bowls for dipping.

Caesar Salad

FOR THE SALAD

½ baguette (about 6 inches), cut into 1½-inch cubes

2 tablespoons olive oil

Kosher salt and black pepper

3 romaine hearts, chopped into 2-inch chunks

8 ounces Parmesan cheese, cut into 16 (½-inch) chunks

FOR THE DRESSING

1 egg yolk

1½ teaspoons Dijon mustard

2 large garlic cloves

1 tablespoon anchovy paste

Juice of 3 lemons

2 teaspoons kosher salt

Black pepper

1⅓ cups olive oil

½ cup grated Parmesan cheese

TO MAKE THE SALAD: Preheat the oven to 400°F.

Place the bread cubes on a baking sheet. Drizzle with the olive oil and season with salt and pepper. Bake for 5 to 7 minutes, or until golden. Remove from the oven and set aside.

Place one chunk of romaine on a skewer, followed by a chunk of Parmesan and a crouton. Repeat this layering process once. Finish the skewer with one more piece of romaine and set it on a platter. Repeat with the remaining ingredients.

TO MAKE THE DRESSING: In a food processor, combine the egg yolk, mustard, garlic, anchovy paste, lemon juice, salt, and pepper to taste and pulse until smooth. With the processor running, slowly pour in the olive oil and process until thick and smooth. Add the cheese and pulse until combined.

Drizzle the dressing over the skewers or serve in small bowls for dipping.

FRESH Corn Pops WITH COMPOUND BUTTERS

A country fair favorite, these are summer on a stick. We offer three different compound butters here, but the possibilities are endless; tap into your inner chef and come up with your own signature combinations based on the herbs and spices you have on hand.

Makes 12 corn pops

Kosher salt

6 ears fresh corn, husked, cleaned, and halved

Lemon-Basil Butter (recipe follows), at room temperature

Smoky Sun-Dried Tomato Butter (recipe follows), at room temperature

Cilantro-Lime Butter (recipe follows), at room temperature

Bring a large pot of salted water to a rolling boil. Add the corn and boil until crisp-tender or a fork pierces a kernel with a little effort, 5 to 8 minutes. Drain.

Using a clean, dry dish towel, hold a corn half and push a 5-inch wooden lollipop stick through one end to create a handle. Repeat with the remaining corn. Serve warm with the softened flavored butters.

Compound Butters

To ¾ cup (1½ sticks) room-temperature **unsalted butter**, stir in:

LEMON-BASIL BUTTER: ¼ cup finely chopped fresh **basil**, 1 finely chopped **scallion**, 2 teaspoons **lemon zest**, and **salt** and **black pepper** to taste.

SMOKY SUN-DRIED TOMATO BUTTER: 3 tablespoons minced **sun-dried tomatoes**, 2 teaspoons **smoked paprika**, ¼ teaspoon **cayenne pepper**, and **salt** and **black pepper** to taste.

CILANTRO-LIME BUTTER: 1 tablespoon each **lime, lemon, and orange zest**; 1 large **garlic** clove, finely grated; 3 tablespoons finely chopped fresh **cilantro**; and **salt** and **black pepper** to taste.

Everything
tastes better
on a SKEWER.

Instead of making ice with water, which eventually dilutes your drink, pour pureed fruits and juices into those trays and add excitement to lemonade or sparkling water. They are pure pleasure on a hot summer day. Use a blender or small food processor to puree the fruit. The ice cubes will keep in the freezer for up to 2 months.

Makes 24 cubes

Fruit ICE CUBES

2 kiwis, peeled and pureed
1 mango, peeled and pureed
1 cup blueberries, pureed
¾ cup fresh orange juice
¾ cup fresh pineapple juice
¾ cup fresh watermelon juice

Pour the individual juices and pureed fruits into ice cube trays and freeze for at least 4 hours. If you want to make layered cubes, fill the wells of the ice cube tray one-quarter to one-third full, then freeze for 2 hours. Remove from the freezer and fill with a different puree or juice, then return to the freezer for another 2 hours. Repeat this process until your trays are filled to the top.

These are somewhat reminiscent of that ice cream truck staple, the strawberry shortcake bar —without all the additives and with a lot less sugar. Of course, you can substitute chocolate ice cream for the strawberry—or any flavor, for that matter.

Makes 8 cupcakes

STRAWBERRY ICE CREAM Cupcakes

1 quart good-quality strawberry ice cream

2 (4 x 8-inch) loaves angel food cake (store-bought or homemade)

2 cups heavy cream, chilled

½ cup sugar

½ vanilla bean, or ½ teaspoon pure vanilla extract

Remove the ice cream from the freezer to soften for about 15 minutes. Cut each cake loaf into 12 thin slices and use a 3-inch round cutter to cut circles from each slice, 24 in total. Place a cake circle in the bottom of each of 8 cups in a muffin tin. Cover the first layer of cake with a layer of the softened ice cream (about ½ inch), spreading it evenly. Place another cake circle on top of the ice cream, pressing to remove any air pockets. Top with more ice cream and a final layer of cake. Place the muffin tin in the freezer for 30 minutes.

Meanwhile, beat the heavy cream in a large bowl for about 3 minutes. If using a vanilla bean, slice the bean in half lengthwise and use the tip of a knife to scrape out the seeds. Slowly add the sugar and vanilla bean seeds (or vanilla extract, if using) to the cream and beat until stiff peaks form.

Once the cupcakes are frozen, turn them out onto a parchment paper–lined baking sheet. You may need to run a paring knife around the edge of each cup to loosen the cakes. Frost each upside-down cupcake with the whipped cream, covering the top and sides. Place on a freezer-proof pan and return to the freezer for 1 hour before serving. The cupcakes will keep in the freezer for up to 2 days.

We've made this for countless summer picnics and parties, much to the delight of kids and adults alike. Pizza—in any iteration—is always popular, especially if it is sweet. Use whatever fruits you like and, if time doesn't allow for making the sugar cookie dough, use brownie mix for the crust.

Makes one 12-inch pizza

sweet pizza with FRUIT TOPPINGS

Sugar Cookie dough (page 159)

1½ (8-ounce) packages cream cheese

2 tablespoons heavy cream

2 tablespoons honey

½ teaspoon orange zest

¼ teaspoon pure vanilla extract

1 kiwi, peeled and sliced

½ cup raspberries

½ cup blueberries

½ cup blackberries

½ cup kumquats, thinly sliced

Preheat the oven to 350°F.

Roll out the dough to about ½ inch thick. Place a 12-inch pizza pan over the dough and, using a paring knife, cut around the edges to make a 12-inch circle. Remove the pan and spray it with cooking spray, then place the dough in the pan. Bake until the edges are golden, about 15 minutes. Set aside to cool.

Combine the cream cheese and heavy cream in a small bowl and, using an electric mixer, mix until creamy and smooth. Add the honey, orange zest, and vanilla and mix until combined. Spread the cream cheese mixture over the cooled cookie, leaving a small border uncovered for the "crust." Arrange the fruits in a design on top of the pizza. Using a very sharp knife, cut the pizza into 12 slices. Serve immediately or chill until ready to serve.

Wagon Wheels and
Meatballs

Garlicky Pull-Aparts

Crispy Asparagus Fries

Tortellini Batons

SEPTEMBER

Sandwich Kebabs

Roasted Vegetable Lasagna Cups

Vegetable Scrabble

Overnight Maple Oatmeal

Every September

we enter the school year with renewed interest in creating healthy, exciting lunches for our kids. Our children were the inspiration for our embarking on food crafting to begin with, and they remain a huge inspiration. As every mother can attest, packing school lunches can be frustrating, especially if those lunches, always made with love and care, come back untouched. (My son is a sneaky one; I know he doesn't eat everything I pack for him, but somehow, the box is empty when he comes home.) But who can blame a kid for not wanting to eat the same old same old? So, with an eye toward both health and excitement, we've created recipes that will sustain burgeoning brains throughout the school day. It's no secret that kids who start the day with a healthy meal are more likely to fare better in school, have less trouble paying attention and fewer disciplinary issues, and enjoy overall better energy and health. But that's all so serious. For the kids' sake, I like to make making lunch fun by having them do much of it with me the night before. Notes left inside their lunchboxes help, too.

school nights

September days are so busy with school, work, and playdates.
There is nothing like comfort food for dinner to bring the
family together at the table, where we can share stories of our
days and recharge for the next one.

WAGON wheels AND meatballs

Gia's Italian roots were the inspiration for this satisfying lunch option. There always seemed to be meatballs and sauce on hand—the Sunday sauce, as it was known in her house, which simmered on the stove all day long.

Yes, you could put piping-hot spaghetti and meatballs on the table and call it dinner, but wouldn't it be more fun to eat out of a jar—maybe outside on the patio to soak up those last days of summer? Ask everyone to grab a jar and a fork and head out the back door. Set a pile of fragrant Garlicky Pull-Aparts (page 188) in the center of the table and savor every second.

Serves 6

RECIPE continues

Continued

FOR THE MEATBALLS

Olive oil

1 tablespoon tomato paste

1 garlic clove, minced

1 large egg

½ teaspoon kosher salt

¼ teaspoon black pepper

1 pound dark meat ground turkey

½ cup Italian bread crumbs

¼ cup grated Parmesan cheese

FOR THE PASTA AND TOMATO SAUCE

1 pound wagon wheel pasta (rotelle)

2 tablespoons extra-virgin olive oil

1 onion, finely chopped

2 garlic cloves, minced

¼ teaspoon red pepper flakes

1½ teaspoons kosher salt

2 tablespoons tomato paste

1 (28-ounce) can crushed tomatoes

1 cup tomato sauce

1 teaspoon dried oregano

½ teaspoon black pepper

⅓ cup chopped fresh basil

TO MAKE THE MEATBALLS: Preheat the oven to 375°F. Brush a nonstick baking sheet with olive oil.

Combine the tomato paste, garlic, egg, salt, and black pepper in a large bowl and stir to mix thoroughly. Add the ground turkey and use your hands to incorporate the seasonings. Add the bread crumbs and cheese and continue mixing until all the ingredients are well blended.

Roll the turkey mixture into 1-tablespoon balls. Place on the prepared baking sheet, brush the tops with olive oil, and bake until cooked through, about 10 minutes.

TO MAKE THE SAUCE AND PASTA: Heat the olive oil in a saucepan over medium heat. Add the onion and cook until fragrant and softened, 2 to 3 minutes. Add the garlic, red pepper flakes, and ½ teaspoon of the salt. Once the onions are translucent, stir in the tomato paste and cook until slightly caramelized, 2 minutes. Add the crushed tomatoes, tomato sauce, and oregano. Season with the black pepper. Reduce the heat to medium-low and simmer for at least 30 minutes, allowing the sauce to thicken. Stir in the fresh basil right before serving.

Bring a large pot of salted water to a boil. Cook the pasta according to the package directions.

Divide the pasta among six small jars. Spoon the sauce and meatballs over and serve immediately.

These delightfully fluffy muffins are the kind of thing you can bake up on even the most hectic night of the week but still look like you spent a long time in the kitchen. The secret is in the prepared buttermilk biscuits. Add fresh garlic, chives, and cheese and you have the perfect accompaniment to pasta.

Makes 12 muffin-size biscuits

GARLICKY Pull-Aparts

2 (12-ounce) tubes chilled buttermilk biscuits (24 biscuits)

5 tablespoons unsalted butter, melted

3 garlic cloves, finely grated

3 tablespoons thinly sliced fresh chives

¼ teaspoon ground black pepper

¼ cup plus 2 tablespoons freshly grated Parmesan cheese

Preheat the oven to 375°F. Lightly grease a 12-cup muffin tin with canola oil.

Cut each biscuit into 4 pieces and set aside. In a large bowl, combine the butter, garlic, chives, pepper, and ¼ cup of the cheese.

Working in batches, brush the dough pieces with the butter mixture, coating them completely. Arrange 8 pieces of dough in each muffin cup, pressing lightly. Sprinkle the tops evenly with the remaining 2 tablespoons cheese.

Bake until the rolls are golden, 14 to 16 minutes. Let cool for 5 minutes before serving.

We brainstormed so many different ways to make a fry that wasn't, well, fried. These were the hands-down winners because they don't hide the vegetable itself, yet they have that all-important crunch that kids love. Gia's son completely fell for them, so much so that whenever she makes them, she makes an extra batch for snacking on.

Serves 4 to 6

CRISPY Asparagus fries

1½ cups panko bread crumbs

2 tablespoons canola oil, plus more for greasing

1 teaspoon garlic powder

1 teaspoon kosher salt

½ teaspoon black pepper

½ cup grated Parmesan cheese

1 large egg

½ cup buttermilk

½ cup all-purpose flour

1 pound medium asparagus spears, tough ends removed

Creamy Dijon mustard, for serving

Preheat the oven to 450°F. Lightly grease a wire rack with canola oil and set it over a baking sheet.

In a shallow bowl, toss the bread crumbs with the 2 tablespoons canola oil, garlic powder, salt, and pepper until well coated; stir in the cheese. In a second shallow bowl, whisk together the egg and buttermilk. Spread the flour in a third shallow bowl. Roll each asparagus spear in flour, then in the egg mixture, letting any excess drip off, and then coat with bread crumbs, pressing gently to adhere.

Arrange the spears on the wire rack and bake until golden brown, about 15 minutes. Serve with a side of Dijon mustard.

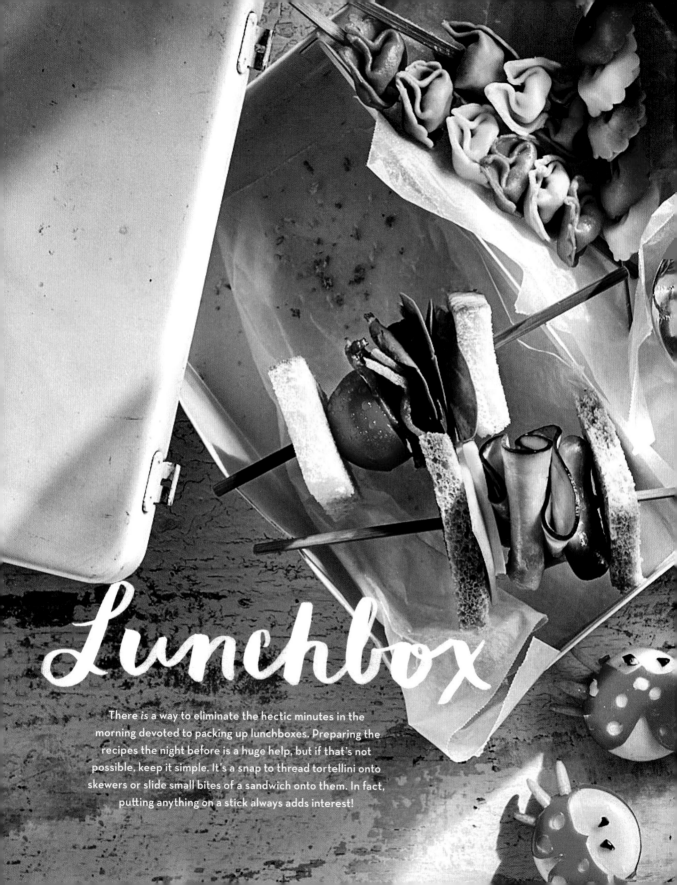

Lunchbox

There *is* a way to eliminate the hectic minutes in the morning devoted to packing up lunchboxes. Preparing the recipes the night before is a huge help, but if that's not possible, keep it simple. It's a snap to thread tortellini onto skewers or slide small bites of a sandwich onto them. In fact, putting anything on a stick always adds interest!

I can say, unapologetically, that the idea of making lunch for my kids is a lovely one, but when it comes right down to it, the actual doing can be a tiny bit annoying. Here's one of my all-time favorite solutions, one that has gone over so well that the kids' lunchtime tablemates have begun to pack these pasta pops, too. Here, the tortellini are served with a basil pesto sauce for dipping, but Tomato Sauce (page 187), warm or at room temperature, also makes a great dipping sauce. Both are excellent for tossing with pasta, too.

Makes 8 skewers and about 1 cup of pesto

Tortellini BATONS

1 (9-ounce) package tortellini

3 cups fresh basil

2 or 3 garlic cloves

2 tablespoons fresh lemon juice

⅔ cup grated Parmesan cheese

⅓ cup pine nuts

¾ cup olive oil

Kosher salt and black pepper

Bring a large pot of salted water to a boil. Cook the tortellini according to the package directions. Drain and set aside to cool.

Meanwhile, in a food processor, combine the basil, garlic, lemon juice, cheese, and pine nuts and pulse to a coarse puree. With the motor running, slowly add the olive oil and process until smooth. Season with salt and pepper.

Slide 4 or 5 tortellini onto each skewer. Pack in a resealable plastic container along with a small container of the basil pesto dipping sauce.

Anything bite-size and displayed or presented in a unique way excites kids—there are so many different sandwich combinations, and you can have a nice array of things for them (and for adults!) to try. Both of my children and Gia's son celebrate their birthdays in September, and these make ideal party fare for a gaggle of school-age kids!

Makes 1

SANDWICH Kebabs

BLT

1 bread slice, toasted and cut into quarters

10 baby spinach leaves

2 cherry tomatoes

2 bacon slices, cooked and broken into large pieces

Mayonnaise (optional), for serving

On a wooden skewer, thread 1 piece of bread, 5 spinach leaves, 1 tomato, half of the bacon, and another bread slice. Repeat with a second skewer. Serve with mayonnaise, if desired.

Ham and Cheese

1 bread slice, toasted and cut into quarters

2 gherkin pickles

2 ham slices

2 cheddar cheese slices, cut into quarters

Dijon mustard (optional), for serving

On a wooden skewer, thread 1 piece of bread, 1 pickle, 1 folded ham slice, half of the cheese, and another piece of bread. Repeat with a second skewer. Serve with mustard, if desired.

ROASTED
VEGETABLE
Lasagna CUPS

Make these on Sunday and packing lunch will be a breeze all week. You can swap out the vegetables for whatever is in season; just be sure to roast them until soft. If you don't have a cutter, you can just cut the noodles into small squares and stack them.

Makes 12 muffin-size lasagnas

RECIPE *continues*

Continued

Kosher salt

Olive oil

½ (1-pound) package lasagna noodles

2 cups cubed (¼-inch) butternut squash

Black pepper

1 eggplant, halved lengthwise and thinly sliced crosswise into half-moons

3 zucchini, thinly sliced crosswise

FOR THE SAUCE

3 cups milk

5 tablespoons unsalted butter

½ teaspoon minced garlic

¼ cup all-purpose flour

½ teaspoon kosher salt

¼ teaspoon black pepper

¼ teaspoon ground nutmeg

¾ cup grated Parmesan cheese

1 cup shredded mozzarella cheese

Bring a large pot of salted water to a boil and add a splash of olive oil. Oil a baking sheet. Cook the pasta in the boiling water for 2 minutes less than directed on the package. Drain and transfer the noodles to the oiled baking sheet, making sure they don't stick together.

Preheat the oven to 375°F. Place the butternut squash on a baking sheet, drizzle with olive oil, and season with salt and pepper. Place the zucchini and eggplant slices on a second baking sheet, drizzle with olive oil, and season with salt and pepper. Roast the zucchini and eggplant until soft, about 15 minutes. Roast the squash for 30 to 35 minutes. Transfer the squash to a bowl and mash with a fork. Set all the vegetables aside.

TO MAKE THE SAUCE: Heat the milk in a saucepan over medium heat, 6 to 8 minutes. In a small skillet, melt the butter with the minced garlic. Add the flour to the butter, whisk to blend, and cook until the mixture bubbles and turns a light golden brown. Ladle in about ½ cup of the hot milk, whisking continuously. Add one more ladle of the milk and whisk until the mixture is smooth. Transfer the mixture to the saucepan with the remainder of the milk, add the salt, pepper, and nutmeg, and whisk thoroughly to blend. The sauce should be thick enough to coat the back of a spoon.

TO ASSEMBLE THE LASAGNA: Use a 2-inch round cutter to cut a total of 48 circles out of the lasagna noodles. Brush a muffin tin with olive oil and place a spoonful of sauce in the bottom of each cup, then top with a noodle. Add a thin layer of mashed squash, then a layer of zucchini and eggplant, and sprinkle with Parmesan. Top with more sauce and another noodle. Repeat the layers, then top with one more noodle, more sauce, and a sprinkle of mozzarella. Bake until the cheese is brown and bubbling, about 25 minutes. Let cool for at least 10 minutes before removing from the cups by running a sharp knife around the rims to loosen.

We love to leave notes in our kids' lunchboxes,
but when we know they are facing a particularly
tough day, we'll take the time to cut out a
message from fresh vegetables.

VEGETABLE
scrabble

Carrots
Cucumbers
Cherry tomatoes
Hummus or ranch dip

Cut the cucumbers and carrots into ½-inch slices on an angle.
Use mini alphabet cutters to cut letters out of the sliced veggies.
Skewer the letters to spell out messages, using cherry tomatoes as
spacers between words. Pack with hummus or ranch dip.

This is in the lunchbox section because it is portable, for those rare (!) times when breakfast is served in the car. There is no more satisfying, sustaining, easy-to-eat-on-the-go morning meal than this.

Any fruit, chopped small, is nice to top off this no-cook oatmeal. Of course, you should substitute your favorite berries, sliced bananas, or diced plums for the pear if you'd like.

Serves 4 little kids or 2 big kids

OVERNIGHT maple oatmeal

2½ cups old-fashioned rolled oats

2 cups whole milk

3 tablespoons maple syrup, plus more for garnish

1 teaspoon pure vanilla extract

½ teaspoon ground cinnamon, plus more for garnish

¼ teaspoon kosher salt

2 small ripe pears, cored and diced

½ cup chopped walnuts, toasted

Vanilla or plain Greek yogurt

In a large bowl, combine the oats, milk, maple syrup, vanilla, cinnamon, and salt. Cover and refrigerate overnight.

Serve the oatmeal buffet-style, with small bowls and jars of the accompaniments—pears, walnuts, yogurt, maple syrup, and cinnamon.

Cran-Apple Witches' Brew

No Bake Honey Pumpkin
Cheesecake Parfaits

Baked Mozzarella Bats

OCTOBER

Mummy Dogs

Orange Jack-o'-Lanterns

Banana Ghosts

Monster Teeth

If ever a holiday

was made for food crafting, Halloween is it. I *LOVE* Halloween. I'm an actor, after all—I wear costumes for a living! We both, of course, can't quite entirely surrender to the candy onslaught that the holiday brings, so we like to have some control over the kids' sugar intake this month. At my house, we practice a ritual that has proven to be so successful that friends have begun to adopt it. Before we leave the house to knock on doors, we allow the kids to pick ten treats from both the treats we baked and special-purchased good-quality chocolates. We label them and stash them in a cupboard. After the kids return with buckets and bags full of candy, they eat the squirreled-away candy and donate what they've collected to the less fortunate. This way, they enjoy the thrill of trick-or-treating but don't suffer the fallout of eating processed junk! Gia's trick is to fill the kids up before they head out—with an open-house style buffet of pasta salads, vegetables, and lots of greens. We do what we can!

Halloween

If you're hosting a pre-trick-or-treat gathering, this menu is perfect. We both insist our kids eat before they head out to ring doorbells, so they won't be tempted to gorge on candy on the run! Among our favorites here are the sausage

A ghastly green drink is essential at a Halloween gathering; to achieve it, we mixed seltzer and natural green food coloring with ginger beer and cranberry juice. We love the idea of serving this in a clear vessel that recalls Dr. Frankenstein's lab, but you could also use a punch bowl (and even float a green ice ring in it by freezing additional green seltzer in a scalloped Bundt pan.)

Serves 16

CRAN-APPLE Witches' Brew

5 cups seltzer and natural green food coloring, chilled

4 cups white cranberry juice cocktail, chilled

2 quarts non-alcoholic ginger beer, chilled

1 orange, thinly sliced

1 green apple, cored and thinly sliced

Stir together all the ingredients in a large punch bowl. Serve over ice. Garnish each drink with an orange slice.

NO BAKE HONEY PUMPKIN Cheesecake Parfaits

Cheesecake, the Italian kind, always signaled a celebration in Gia's childhood home. These were the massive, fluffy rounds that are synonymous with classic Italian pastry shops. When she was growing up, it always meant there was a holiday or special occasion to celebrate.

Makes 8 parfaits

24 gingersnap cookies

1½ cups heavy cream

1½ (8-ounce) packages cream cheese, at room temperature

1 (15-ounce) can pure pumpkin puree

¼ cup honey

1 teaspoon pure vanilla extract

1 teaspoon pumpkin pie spice

¾ cup salted pecans, toasted and chopped

Place the gingersnaps in a resealable plastic bag and roll over them with a rolling pin to crush. You should have about 1½ cups crumbs. Set aside.

In a large bowl, use an electric mixer to beat the cream on high speed until it holds soft peaks. Set aside.

In a food processor, combine the cream cheese, pumpkin, honey, vanilla, and pumpkin pie spice and pulse until very smooth. Scrape the pumpkin mixture into a large bowl and fold in 2 cups of the whipped cream. Spoon the mixture into a gallon-size resealable plastic bag and snip one corner with scissors.

To assemble, spoon 1 heaping tablespoon of the crushed cookies into an 8-ounce glass jar. Pipe in ⅓ cup of the filling and top with a sprinkle of pecans. Repeat with seven more jars.

Cover the parfaits with plastic wrap and refrigerate for at least 2 hours or until well chilled. Top with the remaining whipped cream and, if desired, some additional cookie crumbs, and serve.

Lest young folks are mistaken, mozzarella doesn't come only in the shape of sticks. In fact, when you buy the square block-shaped variety (as opposed to the rounded rectangle), the shapes you can cut it into are endless. A dredging in panko crumbs gives these night creatures their crunch. Bat-shaped cookie cutters can be found at culinary shops and baking supply stores.

Makes 8 bats

BAKED MOZZARELLA Bats

1 (16-ounce) block mozzarella cheese, cut into ½-inch-thick slabs

1½ tablespoons olive oil

1½ cups panko bread crumbs

¼ cup all-purpose flour

2 large eggs

2 teaspoons Italian seasoning

1 teaspoon garlic powder

¼ teaspoon black pepper

1 cup marinara sauce, warmed, for serving

Using a bat-shaped cookie cutter, cut the mozzarella squares into bat shapes, reserving the cheese scraps for another use. Set aside.

Heat the olive oil in a large nonstick skillet over medium-high heat. Add the bread crumbs and sauté, stirring often, until golden brown, about 4 minutes. Set aside to cool.

Line a baking sheet with parchment paper. Place the flour in a shallow bowl. In another shallow bowl, whisk together the eggs and 2 tablespoons water. In a third shallow bowl, combine the toasted bread crumbs, Italian seasoning, garlic powder, and pepper and toss to mix thoroughly. Coat each bat with flour, then dip in the egg mixture, letting any excess drip off, and finally coat with the bread crumb mixture; repeat the egg and the bread crumb coating so that each bat has two layers of breading. As you finish each bat, set them on the prepared baking sheet. Freeze for 30 minutes.

Preheat the oven to 400°F. Bake the bats until just heated through, 6 to 8 minutes. Let stand for 2 minutes before serving with the marinara.

These are the kind of treats that kids go wild for and that parents secretly love to eat. They're an ideal party staple and are also perfect for eating before heading out to ring doorbells.

Makes 12 dogs

Mummy Dogs

1 (11-ounce) tube refrigerated breadstick dough

12 smoked sausage dogs

1 large egg

Small candy eyes (optional)

Mustard, for serving

Preheat the oven to 375°F. Lightly grease a baking sheet with canola oil.

Separate the dough into strips. Using a pizza cutter, cut the dough into ¼- to ½-inch-wide strips. Set aside a couple of strips for the mummies' eyes. Wrap strips of dough around each sausage dog, leaving a ½-inch gap uncovered at about two-thirds of its length for a face. Arrange the wrapped sausage dogs on the prepared baking sheet.

In a small bowl, whisk together the egg and 1 tablespoon water; brush this egg wash over the dough. Bake until golden, 14 to 16 minutes.

Using a toothpick, dab a little dough on the bare part of the sausage for the eyes, then apply a pair of candy eyes on top of the dots, if desired. Serve warm, with a side of mustard.

These are quite a bit more approachable than carving into a huge pumpkin. What's more, you can immediately eat your mistakes and move on. Approach this food craft with your children as you would pumpkin carving—with appropriate supervision.

ORANGE Jack-o'-Lanterns

Assorted oranges

Using an X-ACTO knife, carve a face into the peel of the orange, taking care not to pierce the flesh. Approach it as you would a pumpkin: Carve out clever faces and expressions. Arrange on a buffet table, sideboard, or mantel.

A robe of white chocolate is all it takes to transform a boring old banana into a live creature. Make sure the bananas you use are just firm enough—overripe ones aren't strong enough to carry the white chocolate cloaks, and rock-hard bananas are no fun to bite into.

Makes 4

BANANA GHOSTS

2 bananas, halved crosswise

½ cup white chocolate, melted

8 mini chocolate chips

Insert ice cream sticks into the flat end of each banana. Dip the bananas into the melted white chocolate and apply two mini chocolate chips as each ghost's eyes.

Fake teeth seem to come into our house with regularity: the kind from the novelty store are a repeat gift at birthdays and holidays! Apples, peanut butter, and a few mini marshmallows come together in these hilarious treats, which, needless to say, are among my kids' favorites.

Makes 8

MONSTER TEETH

1 red apple

1 green apple

2 cups mini marshmallows

⅔ cup smooth peanut butter

Quarter each apple, core them, then cut each quarter in half lengthwise to make 8 slices per apple. Spread one side of each slice with peanut butter. Place 6 to 8 marshmallows in a row on the edge of the peanut butter side of half the slices and press another peanut buttered slice on top, forming a mouth. Arrange in a random pattern on a platter to make it look as though the mouths are talking with one another.

Shot Glass Mashed Potatoes

Apple Pie Pops

Individual Spiced Vanilla
Bread Puddings

NOVEMBER

Fresh Apple-Cranberry Sauce

Mini Turkey Potpies

Stuffing Muffins

you might think food crafting should remain outside the realm of Thanksgiving food. For one of the most tradition-bound holidays of the year, it's risky! So we opted, for the most part, to focus on the post-Thanksgiving meal (arguably a favorite of many). That said, there *is* apple pie on a stick. Yes, you can put a "piece" of pie on a stick by gathering pie dough spread with apple filling up into a pouch around a stick. This is how the food crafter's mind works! There are also indulgent bread puddings made in individual ramekins that can hold their own on the Thanksgiving dessert buffet. Perhaps some of our proudest creations are the most popular: muffins made with leftover stuffing, and tiny turkey potpies.

Thanksgiving

My Thanksgiving involves an ever-changing group that always includes my family, of course, and anyone who can't get home for the holidays. The open-door policy lasts the entire weekend, which means I need to have plenty of leftovers on hand. Gia's large extended family, all of whom share the belief that food is love, would rather be in the kitchen than anywhere else on Thanksgiving. Each family has its own signature dish, and now Gia's son and his cousins are in charge of the post-Thanksgiving spread. That's where these food crafting recipes come in.

Makes about 6 servings

SHOT GLASS Mashed Potatoes

1 teaspoon kosher salt, plus more as needed

1½ pounds Yukon Gold potatoes, peeled and quartered

3 tablespoons unsalted butter

4 to 5 tablespoons half-and-half

Black pepper

Sour cream, for garnish

Chopped fresh chives, for garnish

Cooked bacon, crumbled, for garnish

Blue cheese, crumbled, for garnish

Fill a large pot three-quarters full with cold water. Add the salt and potatoes and bring the water to a boil over high heat. Reduce the heat to medium and cook for 15 minutes, or until the potatoes are easily pierced with a fork. Drain and transfer to a large bowl. Using an electric mixer, whip the potatoes, adding the butter and half-and-half gradually, thoroughly mixing after each addition. Season with salt and pepper. Working in batches if necessary, spoon the potatoes into a piping bag fitted with a decorative tip and pipe into clear shot glasses (or juice glasses, if you'd rather). Garnish as desired and serve.

This technique works for any filled pie; just be sure to pinch the dough tightly around the stick.

Makes 6 pops

Apple Pie Pops

- 4 tablespoons (½ stick) unsalted butter
- 2 large Granny Smith apples, peeled, cored, and diced
- 2 teaspoons fresh lemon juice
- ¼ cup packed brown sugar
- ¼ teaspoon ground cinnamon
- ¼ teaspoon kosher salt
- 1 refrigerated rolled piecrust
- 1 egg white, lightly beaten

Melt the butter in a small skillet over medium heat. Add the apples, lemon juice, brown sugar, cinnamon, and salt and stir to combine. Cook until the sugar has melted and the apples have softened, about 10 minutes. Remove from the heat and let cool.

Preheat the oven to 350°F. Line a baking sheet with parchment paper.

Place the pie dough on a work surface and use a 3-inch round cutter to cut 12 circles from the dough, rerolling the dough scraps as needed. Place 6 of the circles on the prepared baking sheet and place an ice cream stick into the center of each circle. Scoop a heaping tablespoon of the apple mixture into the center of each circle on top of the stick. Brush the edges of the dough with egg white and top with another circle of dough. Use a fork to press and seal the edges, making sure to seal around the stick. Use a paring knife to make a small slit in the center of each pie to allow steam to escape. Bake for 18 to 20 minutes, or until the crust is golden. Let cool slightly before serving, as the filling will be hot!

These are wonderful to put out on the Thanksgiving dessert spread and are lovely served warm or at room temperature. Double the recipe—you'll want to have some on hand over the weekend.

Makes 8 servings

INDIVIDUAL SPICED VANILLA bread puddings

4 large eggs

¾ cup granulated sugar

1½ cups half-and-half

1 teaspoon pure vanilla extract

1 vanilla bean, split lengthwise and seeds scraped

½ teaspoon ground cinnamon

⅛ teaspoon ground nutmeg

4 cups cubed (1½-inch) brioche

Confectioners' sugar, for dusting

Preheat the oven to 375°F. Spray eight ½-cup ramekins with cooking spray.

In a large bowl, use an electric mixer to beat the eggs on low speed until frothy. Add the granulated sugar and beat until well blended. Add the half-and-half, the vanilla extract, vanilla bean seeds, cinnamon, and nutmeg and beat on low speed until incorporated. Fill the prepared ramekins with bread cubes. Pour the egg mixture into each ramekin, filling them evenly to the rim.

Place the ramekins in a large baking dish and pour boiling water into the dish until it reaches about halfway up the ramekins, making sure not to get water in the ramekins. Carefully transfer to the oven and bake for 25 minutes, or until a toothpick inserted into the center of the pudding comes out clean. Remove from the oven and let cool. Dust with confectioners' sugar before serving.

I love bagels. There, I said it. I eat gluten . . . and I live in LA!!!! We have been known to mail-order bagels from my favorite place in New York, H&H Bagels, for the post-Thanksgiving sandwich extravaganza. Gia takes her cues from her Italian roots and uses ciabatta bread, layering the contents of the meal between the loaf, wrapping it, weighting it with a heavy pan, and refrigerating it overnight. The next day, there are chilled pressed sandwiches to eat. Whatever way you choose to make them, turkey sandwiches are a must, and they are nothing without a good dollop of cranberry sauce. The sauce is also delicious on Stuffing Muffins (page 232). It will keep, tightly covered, in the refrigerator for up to 2 weeks.

Makes 2 cups, to serve 8

FRESH
apple-cranberry sauce

1 (12-ounce) package fresh or frozen cranberries

¾ cup sugar

2 teaspoons orange zest

½ cup fresh orange juice

1 small green apple, peeled, cored, and finely chopped

In a medium saucepan, combine the cranberries, sugar, orange zest, orange juice, and ¼ cup water and bring to a boil over medium heat. Reduce the heat to medium-low and simmer, stirring occasionally, for 10 minutes. Stir in the apple and cook for 5 to 10 minutes more, or until the cranberries have popped and the mixture has slightly thickened. Let cool completely, then cover tightly and refrigerate for at least 4 hours or up to 3 days.

MINI turkey POTPIES

Potpie is the ultimate day-after-Thanksgiving dish. Making mini versions is just as easy as preparing one large pie, and it allows you to unleash your creativity on the crusts; try a lattice pattern or use cookie cutters to stamp out fun shapes. Use 6-ounce Weck jars to make these.

Makes 12 potpies

4 tablespoons (½ stick) unsalted butter

1 sweet onion, finely chopped

1 cup packed shredded carrots

1 cup chopped mushrooms

¼ cup all-purpose flour

1½ cups whole milk

1½ cups chicken broth

2½ cups diced cooked turkey

¾ cup frozen peas

¼ cup chopped fresh parsley

2 teaspoons finely chopped fresh thyme

Kosher salt and black pepper

2 (14.1-ounce) packages refrigerated rolled piecrusts (4 rolls)

1 large egg yolk, well beaten

In a large Dutch oven, melt the butter over medium-high heat; add the onion, carrots, and mushrooms and sauté for 5 minutes, or until tender. Sprinkle the vegetables with the flour and cook, stirring continuously, for 1 minute. Gradually whisk in the milk and broth and bring to a boil, whisking often. Stir in the turkey, peas, and herbs and simmer for 5 minutes more, or until thickened. Season with salt and pepper. Let cool.

Meanwhile, lightly roll out 2 piecrusts and cut each one into 6 pieces. Line twelve 6-ounce Weck jars with the dough, pressing and tearing to patch and cover all sides of the jars. Roll out and cut the remaining the 2 piecrusts into 12 rounds slightly larger than the opening of the jars.

Spoon the cooled filling into the jars. Top each jar with a dough round, folding the edges under, then seal with a fork around the edges. Cut a few vents in the center with the tip of a knife to allow steam to escape. In a small bowl, beat the egg yolk with 2 teaspoons water and brush the dough tops with this egg wash. Freeze for 15 minutes.

While the pies are in the freezer, preheat the oven 400°F. Line a baking sheet with parchment paper. Place the jars on the prepared baking sheet and bake for 30 to 35 minutes, until the crust is golden brown. Let cool slightly before serving.

Because who wouldn't want a savory muffin made from the big day's stuffing??? The best part? Making them in tins means there are more crispy edges—no elbowing others out of the way for them!

Makes 12 muffins

Stuffing MUFFINS

- 5 cups ½-inch pieces day-old white bread
- 6 tablespoons (¾ stick) unsalted butter, plus more for the muffin tin
- 1½ cups diced onions
- ¾ cup chopped celery
- ½ cup fresh flat-leaf parsley, chopped
- 1 tablespoon chopped fresh sage
- 2 teaspoons fresh thyme
- 1 teaspoon kosher salt
- ½ teaspoon black pepper
- 1¼ cups chicken broth
- 1 large egg

Preheat the oven to 250°F. Grease a 12-cup muffin tin with butter. Place the bread pieces in a single layer on a baking sheet and bake for about 1 hour, until dried out. Let cool. Transfer the cooled bread to a large bowl. Raise the oven temperature to 350°F.

In a skillet, melt the butter over medium heat. Add the onions and celery and cook until soft, about 8 minutes. Transfer to the bowl with the bread and mix to combine. Add the herbs, salt, and pepper and toss to combine. Slowly add half the broth and toss.

In a separate bowl, combine the remaining broth and egg and whisk to blend. Add the egg mixture to the bread and seasoning and fold until incorporated. Place an ice cream scoop full of the stuffing mixture into each cup of the prepared muffin tin. Cover with aluminum foil and bake for 20 minutes, then uncover and bake for 10 to 15 minutes more, or until the tops are golden.

Latkes on a Stick
Candy Cane Cupcakes
Vanilla-Peppermint Hot Chocolate
Snowflake Pizzas
Gingerbread Loaves
Snowy Holiday Terrarium

DECEMBER

Cheese Fondue with
Star Dippers
Sparkling Mocktails
Truffle Parmesan Risotto
Ricotta & Spaghetti Squash Cupcakes
Glitter Cake Pops

Yes, we can talk about

the equal parts joy and stress
this month brings. I often refer
to. it as the season in which I need to give a lot of gifts. Gia plugs in the basement
refrigerator in anticipation of the family that descends on her, always, always bearing
Proustian dishes and treats that bring childhood Christmas memories flooding back.

There are clever ways to up the fun quotient and lower the pressure. I do bake
days, in which friends and their families gather in my kitchen and bake...and bake and
bake. At the end of the day, everyone leaves with an armload of edible gifts for giving.
The gang also puts aside a large bundle of gifts for the less fortunate.

Gia hosts the traditional Italian Christmas Eve Feast of the Seven Fishes, in which
there are that many dishes on the menu, all featuring fish.

For the dozens of gatherings and celebrations that seem to lead up to these epic days, there are simple, sweet things to make that *everyone*—kids, adults, grinches—loves. Show me one person who doesn't want to eat pizza, hot chocolate, or cupcakes! They're the kind of treats that you can pull together without a whole lot of fanfare.

Latkes ON A Stick

This is Gia's mother-in-law's family recipe and a staple on her family's holiday table. She's hoping that her son will continue the tradition when he grows up.

Makes 16 potato pancakes

RECIPE continues

Continued

2½ pounds baking potatoes, peeled

1 small onion

2 large eggs, slightly beaten

2 to 3 tablespoons all-purpose flour or matzo meal

¼ teaspoon baking powder

1 teaspoon kosher salt

Vegetable oil, for frying

Applesauce, for serving

Sour cream, for serving

Shred the potatoes using the shredding blade of a food processor or by hand on the large holes of a box grater. Place the shreds in a colander. (If the shreds are large, fit the food processor with the metal S-blade and process the potatoes in batches to chop them a bit more.)

Shred or finely chop the onion. Add the onion to the potatoes and allow the onion-potato mixture to drain in the sink for 10 minutes. Rinse and transfer the mixture to a clean dish towel and wring out the excess moisture.

Put the potato mixture in a bowl and add the eggs, 2 tablespoons of flour, the baking powder, and the salt. Mix well. If the batter is thin and won't hold its shape, add the additional tablespoon of flour.

In a large skillet, heat 1 inch of oil over medium-high heat. Using a slotted spoon, place about 2 tablespoons of the potato mixture into the hot oil for each pancake. Do not crowd the pan.

Flatten the pancakes slightly with the back of the spoon and fry until golden on both sides, turning once. Transfer to paper towels to drain. The pancakes may be kept warm in a low oven in single layer.

Before serving, push a lollipop stick into the edge of each latke. Serve with applesauce and sour cream.

The latkes can be frozen for serving later. Arrange them in a single layer on a baking sheet and put them in the freezer. Once frozen, stack them in layers in a rigid container and cover tightly to store. When ready to use, return the frozen pancakes to baking sheets in single layers. Bake at 450°F for 5 to 10 minutes, or until crisp and bubbling.

Consider the vanilla cupcake a blank canvas—you can put any crushed holiday candy on top; candy canes are the most iconic, but there's also peppermint pretzel bark, ribbon candy, or even crushed nuts.

Makes 12 cupcakes

Candy Cane Cupcakes

1 (15.25-ounce) box vanilla cake mix

1¼ teaspoons peppermint extract

Vanilla Buttercream (page 26)

6 candy canes

Preheat the oven according to the cake mix package directions. Line a 12-cup muffin tin with festive paper liners.

Prepare the cake batter according to the package directions, adding ¾ teaspoon of the peppermint extract. Whisk to blend. Evenly distribute the batter in the prepared muffin tin. Bake the cupcakes for 15 to 17 minutes, or until the tops are golden and a toothpick inserted into the center comes out clean. Let cool.

Meanwhile, combine the buttercream with the remaining ¾ teaspoon peppermint extract and whisk to combine. Use a rolling pin or the bottom of a cup to crush the candy canes. Frost the top of each cupcake and sprinkle with the crushed candy.

A fragrant rim of crushed peppermint stick flavors every sip of this delicious holiday staple.

Serves 8

VANILLA-PEPPERMINT hot chocolate

- 2 tablespoons Dutch-process cocoa powder
- 8 cups milk
- 10 sprigs fresh mint
- 2 vanilla beans, halved lengthwise and seeds scraped out, or 1 teaspoon pure vanilla extract
- 8 ounces semisweet chocolate, finely chopped
- 8 ounces milk chocolate, finely chopped
- 4 candy canes, finely crushed
- Marshmallows or whipped cream, for serving

Bring ½ cup water to a simmer in a large saucepan over medium heat. Add the cocoa powder and whisk until smooth. Pour in the milk and whisk until combined. Add the mint and vanilla bean pods and seeds and bring to a simmer; after 10 minutes, remove the mint and vanilla bean pods and discard. Add the semisweet and milk chocolates and whisk continuously until the chocolate has melted and the mixture is frothy and smooth.

Run a wet paper towel along the rims of eight mugs. Place the crushed candy canes on a small plate and press the wet rims of the mugs into the candy. Pour the hot chocolate into the prepared mugs and serve with marshmallows or a dollop of whipped cream.

Look for at least a 3-inch snowflake cookie cutter to make these personal pizzas. Prepare the dough before you go out for a walk and bake them when you return to warm yourself with hot chocolate.

Serves 6 to 8

snowflake PIZZAS

FOR THE DOUGH

- 1 teaspoon sugar
- 1 cup warm water
- 1 (¼-ounce) packet active dry yeast
- 1 cup whole wheat flour
- 1¼ cups all-purpose flour
- ½ cup semolina
- 1 teaspoon kosher salt
- 2 tablespoons olive oil
- ½ cup cornmeal

FOR THE TOPPINGS

- 1 cup Tomato Sauce (see page 187)
- 2 cups shredded mozzarella cheese
- ⅓ cup thinly sliced mushrooms
- ½ cup spinach or other hearty greens, coarsely chopped

TO MAKE THE DOUGH: In a measuring cup, dissolve the sugar in the warm water, then stir in the yeast. Let the mixture rest until foamy, about 5 minutes. In the bowl of a stand mixer fitted with the dough hook, combine the flours, semolina, and salt and mix on low speed to combine. Pour in the olive oil and the yeast mixture and mix on medium speed until the dough gathers into a ball. Transfer the dough to an oiled bowl and cover with plastic wrap. Let the dough rest on the counter until it has doubled in size, about 45 minutes.

TO ASSEMBLE THE PIZZAS: Preheat the oven to 400°F. Sprinkle two baking sheets evenly with the cornmeal. On a well-floured work surface, roll out the dough to ½-inch thickness. Use a snowflake cutter to cut individual pizzas and transfer them to the prepared baking sheets. Spoon sauce over the dough and sprinkle with cheese and toppings. Bake until the crust is golden and the cheese is bubbling, about 7 minutes.

Prepare multiples of these to give as parting gifts to unexpected visitors. Bake them in disposable aluminum or ovenproof paper pans, let them cool, and then slip them into glassine or parchment paper bags, and tie with decorative ribbon.

Makes two 8 x 4-inch loaves

gingerbread LOAVES

2 cups all-purpose flour

⅓ cup minced crystallized ginger

1 teaspoon baking soda

½ teaspoon baking powder

½ teaspoon kosher salt

1 teaspoon ground cinnamon

½ teaspoon ground nutmeg

½ teaspoon ground ginger

¼ teaspoon ground cloves

¾ cup (1½ sticks) unsalted butter

1½ cups packed dark brown sugar

2 large eggs

1 (15-ounce) can pure pumpkin puree

⅓ cup molasses

Confectioners' sugar, for garnish (optional)

Preheat the oven to 325°F. Grease and flour two 8 x 4-inch loaf pans.

In a large bowl, stir together the flour, crystallized ginger, baking soda, baking powder, salt, and spices.

In the bowl of a stand mixer fitted with the paddle attachment, beat the butter at medium speed until creamy. Add the brown sugar and beat until fluffy. Add the eggs one at a time; beat until well blended after each addition. Add the pumpkin and molasses and beat until combined (the mixture will look curdled–this is okay). Add the flour mixture to the butter mixture and beat at low speed until blended.

Divide the batter evenly between the prepared loaf pans. Bake for 1 hour 20 minutes or until a toothpick inserted into the center comes out clean. Let cool in the pans for 10 minutes, then remove from the pans and set on a wire rack to cool completely. Dust with confectioners' sugar, if desired. The loaves will keep, tightly covered, at room temperature for up to 3 days; they can also be double wrapped in plastic wrap, sealed in freezer bags, and frozen for up to 2 weeks.

Gather up these ingredients and use our version simply as a guide. This makes a wonderful centerpiece on the dining room table, on a side table in the entry hall, or even in the front window.

Makes 4 to 5 terrariums, depending on jar size

Snowy Holiday Terrarium

2 Gingerbread Loaves (page 245), crumbled

5 to 7 gingerbread man cookies, packaged or bakery-bought

Fresh rosemary sprigs

Sweetened flaked coconut

Candy canes

Round peppermints

Tiny holiday figurines, for garnish

Divide the crumbled gingerbread into variously sized cookie or mason jars with wide mouths so that it reaches about one-third of the way up the jar. Set the cookies into the cake, pressing lightly to secure. Arrange the rosemary sprigs around the cookies to mimic trees and bushes. Sprinkle the coconut over it all for snow. Decorate with candy canes and peppermints and garnish with a few figurines, if desired.

New Year's Eve

These days, it's almost impossible for either of us to stay up to the stroke of midnight—the evening is more Scrabble than sequins. But celebrating the end of the year with great fanfare is still important to us. It's a perfect holiday for food crafting: sparkling champagne, pretty mocktails, and an elegant meal. Start with a convivial fondue with star-shaped apples and baguette slices for dipping. Drizzle truffle oil over a creamy risotto and serve it with pretty, savory cupcakes. When the dinner dishes disappear, bring out a tray of gorgeous, glittery cake pops. Happy New Year!

This is an instant conversation starter; everyone loves to dip into the fragrant, melted, gooey cheese! You can also serve this with roasted peewee potatoes, blanched broccoli, and asparagus spears.

Serves 8

Cheese fondue with STAR DIPPERS

2 tablespoons cornstarch

½ teaspoon dry mustard

Dash of ground nutmeg

1¾ cups dry white wine

10 ounces Swiss or Emmentaler cheese, shredded

10 ounces Gruyère cheese, shredded

Apples and baguette, for dipping

In a small bowl, stir together the cornstarch, mustard, nutmeg, and 1 tablespoon water; set aside.

In a heavy pot, bring the wine to a simmer over medium heat. Add the cheeses to the simmering wine in several batches, stirring continuously to melt. Once the cheese has just melted, stir in the cornstarch mixture and bring to a simmer. Cook for 5 minutes more, or until the fondue is thick and smooth. Transfer to a fondue pot and keep warm over a flame.

Use small star cutters to cut apple and baguette slices into stars. Place them on skewers and dip in the fondue.

So lovely and so inclusive—even the children can toast with these pretty drinks.

Serves 8

Sparkling MOCKTAILS

Edible glitter or colored sparkling sugar

1½ cups pear nectar

¾ cup pomegranate juice

¾ cup blood orange juice

1 bottle sparkling cider or champagne for the grown-ups

Run a wet paper towel along the rims of eight champagne flutes. Place edible glitter onto a small plate and roll the wet rims in the glitter to coat. Set aside.

About 1 hour before guests arrive, in a pitcher, combine the pear nectar, pomegranate juice, and blood orange juice, stir, and chill. Pour the juice mixture into the prepared champagne flutes to fill them about halfway. Top each with chilled sparkling cider.

By simply drizzling a little truffle oil over this comforting risotto, you've dressed it up for New Year's Eve. Skip the truffle topping for a cozy weeknight meal and instead, top it with roasted vegetables and rotisserie chicken.

Serves 8

TRUFFLE PARMESAN risotto

- 5 cups chicken broth
- 2 tablespoons olive oil
- 2½ cups Arborio rice
- 1 cup dry white wine
- 1 teaspoon kosher salt
- ½ cup freshly grated Parmesan cheese
- ½ cup freshly grated Fontina cheese
- ¼ cup chopped fresh parsley
- ½ teaspoon black pepper

  Truffle oil, for drizzling

Bring the broth and 4 cups water to a simmer in a large saucepan over low heat.

In a Dutch oven or large saucepan, heat the olive oil over medium-high heat. Add the rice and sauté for 1 minute. Reduce the heat to medium. Add the wine and salt and cook, stirring often, until the liquid has been absorbed. Add 1 cup of the hot broth mixture; cook, stirring often, until the liquid has been absorbed. Repeat the procedure with the remaining broth mixture, 1 cup at a time. (The total cooking time will be about 30 minutes.)

Once the rice is softened and creamy, stir in the cheeses, parsley, pepper, and a drizzle of truffle oil. Serve immediately.

These are wonderfully moist and hearty; feel free to substitute different cheeses or the sauce we make for Wagon Wheels with Meatballs (page 187) for the ricotta mixture.

Makes 12 "cupcakes"

RICOTTA AND spaghetti squash CUPCAKES

- 1 (3- to 3½-pound) spaghetti squash, halved lengthwise and seeded
- 2 large eggs
- ⅔ cup freshly grated Parmesan cheese
- Kosher salt and black pepper
- 1½ cups ricotta cheese
- ¼ cup chopped fresh basil, plus more torn leaves for garnish
- 6 grape tomatoes, halved

Preheat the oven to 375°F. Lightly grease a 12-cup muffin tin with canola oil and line the cups with 5-inch squares of parchment paper (or use cupcake liners). Lightly grease a baking sheet. Bake the squash, cut sides down, on the baking sheet for 30 minutes, or until the flesh is tender. Let cool slightly, then scrape the inside of the squash with a fork to remove spaghetti-like strands. Reduce the oven temperature to 350°F.

In a large bowl, whisk together the eggs and ⅓ cup of the Parmesan. Gently fold in the squash and season with salt and pepper. In a separate bowl, stir together the remaining ⅓ cup Parmesan, the ricotta, and the basil and season with salt and pepper.

Divide the squash mixture among the prepared muffin cups, making a slight indentation in the center of the squash. Bake until set, 15 to 20 minutes. Dollop a spoonful of the ricotta mixture in the center of each muffin and bake for 5 minutes more.

Top each cupcake with the grape tomatoes and torn basil leaves and serve.

so
HEALTHY,
so
satisfying

These glamorous little sweets are dressed perfectly for ringing in the New Year. Edible glitter is available in baking supply stores and some gourmet supermarkets.

Makes 24 pops

glitter CAKE POPS

1 (15.25-ounce) box chocolate or vanilla cake mix

Vanilla Buttercream (page 26)

10 ounces white chocolate

Edible glitter or metallic sprinkles

Preheat the oven according to the cake mix package directions. Line a baking sheet with parchment paper. Prepare and bake the cake according to the package directions. Let cool completely, then use your hands to break the cake over a large bowl until you have large crumbs. Add the frosting a few dollops at a time and mix until fully incorporated. You only need enough frosting to create a doughlike consistency that can be molded.

Roll the "dough" into tablespoon-size balls and place on the parchment paper–lined baking sheet. Freeze for 45 minutes.

Melt a handful of the chocolate in a small bowl in the microwave or in a heatproof bowl set over a pan of gently boiling water. Remove the balls from the freezer. Dip lollipop sticks into the melted chocolate and insert one stick into the center of each ball. The melted chocolate will act as an adhesive. Return the pops to the freezer for 10 minutes.

Melt the remaining chocolate. Remove the pops from the freezer and dip them into the melted chocolate, using a spoon to spread the chocolate, fully covering the surface. Sprinkle with edible glitter and return to the baking sheet to set.

Acknowledgments

There are so many people who
helped us create and "craft" this book,
and they all deserve a thank-you.

First of all, **AMY NEUNSINGER**, none of this would have been possible without you. You took all our crazy ideas and turned them into art. You also managed to make taking pictures easy for two women who do not like having their pictures taken.

Thank you to our amazing team at GRAND CENTRAL! You turned our vision into a reality.

BRIAN BOONE, for helping us create the world we wanted our pictures to live in.

Thank you to the best "Pretty Committee" ever: DAVID DeLEON, ALI SHERRY, and TARA SWEENEN, we love your guts.

WILL COPENHAVER, and everyone at LE CREUSET, thank you for making the best cookware and bakeware and always being so generous.

SYLVIA from FOOSE, for donating all the incredible cookie cutters.

BETH KATZ from MT. WASHINGTON POTTERY, your incredible pottery made every recipe shine.

KEVIN YORN and all the incredible lawyers at Morris/Yorn, thank you for working tirelessly.

KATHLEEN HACKETT, thank you for helping us to organize our thoughts into cohesive sentences.

MARIAN COOPER-CAIRNS (AND TEAM), thank you for making our food look more beautiful than it probably has a right to.

AUDRIANA RUSSO, our backbone...your culinary genius inspires us daily. We love you!

Thank you to OUR FAMILIES, for putting up with the madness that is a book shoot.

And lastly, to our other partner, GALIT LAIBOW, for encouraging (well, pushing) us to realize our dream of this book.

Okay, and really last—thank you to ALL OF YOU for purchasing this book and having fun with food.

Note: *Italic* page numbers refer to photographs.

V

W

Y

ABOUT the Authors

SARAH MICHELLE GELLAR is a Golden Globe nominee and Emmy–winning actress best known for her roles in *Buffy the Vampire Slayer*, ABC's *All My Children*, CBS's *The Crazy Ones*, and the movies *Cruel Intentions* and *The Grudge*, among others. Off-screen, Gellar lends her time and support to child and hunger organizations as an advocate and activist. She works closely with No Kid Hungry and Good+ Foundation.

In October 2015, Gellar stepped into a new role as entrepreneur, cofounding Foodstirs (www.foodstirs.com) along with Galit Laibow and Gia Russo. Foodstirs is an organic line of quick scratch baking mixes and kits that aims to modernize traditional baking and bring families together in the kitchen. Foodstirs inspires creativity and curiosity while emphasizing the importance of a healthier lifestyle. Sarah's best role to date is as mother to her two children.

GIA RUSSO grew up in an Italian household where cooking and entertaining played an integral role in her childhood. This passion led her to a career with *Martha Stewart Living*, where Gia created original content and developed products. She later went on to form her own lifestyle brand, MiGi. Gia coauthored three bestselling entertaining/ cookbooks and gained national recognition on *The Oprah Winfrey Show*.

Her creative vision and branding expertise led her to work with large brands such as Crate & Barrel, Williams-Sonoma, Pottery Barn Kids, and Pepperidge Farm. Gia has contributed to hundreds of magazines, websites, and TV shows, which created a consumer following within the mom demographic. Gia joined forces with Galit Laibow and Sarah Michelle Gellar to launch Foodstirs, a modern baking company. Her passions are her family and her two French bulldogs.